WHAT TO DO WHEN
YOU'RE
DEAD

WHAT TO DO WHEN YOU'RE DEAD

*A Former Atheist Interviews
the Source of Infinite Being*

SONDRA SNEED

RAINBOW RIDGE
BOOKS

133.93

Sne

Rainbow Ridge Books

Copyright © 2013 by Sondra Sneed

Cover and interior design by Frame25 Productions
Cover photo © AVTG/iStockphoto

Published by:
Rainbow Ridge Books, LLC
140 Rainbow Ridge Road
Faber, Virginia 22938
434-361-1723

If you are unable to order this book from your local
bookseller, you may order directly from the distributor.

Square One Publishers, Inc.
115 Herricks Road
Garden City Park, NY 11040
Phone: (516) 535-2010
Fax: (516) 535-2014
Toll-free: 877-900-BOOK

Visit the author at:
www.SondraSneed.com

Library of Congress Cataloging-in-Publication Data applied for.

ISBN 978-1-937907-11-2

10 9 8 7 6 5 4 3 2 1

Printed on acid-free recycled paper
in the United States of America

This is for my Father, Harold Leroy Sneed, a man whose ironclad will in the face of unfortunate circumstances taught me strength and courage to use what the good Lord gave me.

Acknowledgements

You, the reader, are the first one I wish to thank, because you are willing to take a chance on your mind's ability to deepen. Depth is a virtue I hold dear and now I get a chance to share this depth with another mortal mind. Without you I would not have a purpose in this world. The only reason I came here, to Earth, as you will discover, is to give God back to humankind, and also to take back our God-given power to create from the hands of greedy men. The pages forthcoming will explain how this is so. My gratitude extends to those who have taught me the value of my God-given gift. Too numerous to mention, these people have allowed me to conduct personal readings and facilitate a dialogue with God using my pen to document each session. In these documents God has taught me that every single human being is connected to their most high being, and God can give each person access just by making their mind open and receptive to God's advice. This is a precious undertaking that reveals such private, spiritual detail. I am honored to be one whom they have trusted to open that door.

On a personal level, I have others to thank who have made this day possible. First my beloved husband, Dee Brown, who has given me room to move in the mind of God. While he loves to play dictator over the household, he is a gentle partner in my creativity, and probably my biggest fan. He is a lion tamer to the beast in me and gives me solace from the outside world as he treasures my heart and honors the dictates of my soul. We cling to each other in such a healthy way that I often say he is the tree to my orchid. His kisses before leaving each morning wake me with tender love. I was 40 when we met; he was worth the wait. I claim his son, Cody for my own, grateful for my chance at domestic normalcy. I never imagined it would be so lovely.

I am deeply grateful to the bookmakers and sellers who will take this work beyond my spiral notebooks, making it possible to share God's words with the world, where they belong. Namely Robert Friedman who has taken the chance that people are ready for the news God discloses in this book. Robert's experience in publishing this kind of spiritual dictation makes him a Master in my eyes. I can't think of a better publisher I could have found, knowing he has traversed this path before. I also want to thank Carole Hill for her help in transcribing and editing my handwritten manuscript; it is an effort she takes seriously, as do I. Others who have been influential in the process of my going public are Jess Todtfeld, Steve Harrison, and Ginny Shepard. Their belief in me, and in this message, gave me faith when it was waning. They are cheerleaders who inspire so many to reach beyond the comfort zone of an average life.

I also want to thank Dr. Robert Sanders in Kansas City who donated time to counsel me when I was broke and suffering cyclical depression while in my twenties. I never had a chance to thank him enough. And AleXis Hurley who helped me step my first step on this publishing journey and without whom I would be less sure footed when the time came to write this book. Catherine Day, Robert Sneed, Patricia Sneed, Jeanette Brown, Ilhwa Compton—family members all; I rely heavily on their open-minded acceptance to keep me connected to the ground. I want to thank my mother, Dee Ann Yokpore, who did not raise me, but reserved a place for me in her heart for when the time came that we would meet again. I thank the women who took her place, and wish I had shown them more appreciation.

I want to thank my Grandma and Grandpa for sweet childhood memories. I felt loved unconditionally; they were always glad to see me. I miss them terribly sometimes.

But most of all, I want to thank my Dad. He suffered so much in life from situations he seemed unprepared to manage. Nevertheless, he did manage them. He has said, in the hard times, "People say everything happens for the best, but that's not true, you make the best of a bad situation." His powerful will rubbed off on me, and I've never given-up on anything I wanted to accomplish, no matter how hard, thanks to him.

I see a glimmer of my Dad in my best girlfriend, Lisa Hampton-Ashabranner, senior geologist, former dancer, and mother of three. Since college we have had parallel lives where we've inspired and supported each other. For twenty-three years her faith in me has never waned, nor mine in her. I didn't marry until I was 42 because of her. Before my husband, I just couldn't find someone who thought as highly of me as she had all those years. She's the one who set us up, and made a good bet that day.

In closing, I wish to acknowledge all of God's messengers who have come before me, many of whom I mention in the introduction. Their bravery is a landmark I use whenever I question my ability to face the difficulties that come when revealing truth and wisdom.

Table of Contents

Introduction

What you are looking for is what is looking.
—St. Francis of Assisi

How do you introduce God? There are moments I feel completely unprepared to represent a book that has taken me seven years to summon the courage to write. The only reason I write it now is because I have found that if one hides from purpose long enough, one's work in the world has no meaning whatsoever. The need to make a buck loses its luster and if you don't get on with it, that is get on with the reason you were born, you might as well end your existence, because you're just taking up precious space on an over-populated planet. To introduce this book, a book written as a message from God to the world of mankind, I first have to address the obvious question: How do I know I am talking to God?

As a former atheist I don't have a simple response. The question implies I should know what God is, and I can compare that knowledge with the dialogue I am having in this book. The Being with which this book converses says, "God is what God makes as God becomes." I find this consistent with the Hebrew narrative, when Moses asked God's name. God replied, "Ehyeh asher ehyeh," which is translated "I am that I am," but it also has been translated as, "I shall be that I shall be."

I don't refer to God in pronoun—He nor She—because God insists gender is a false way of describing God's nature and being. The he/she distraction we place on men and women is also false, because we are a generic gender in soul/spirit form, which will be discussed further in the book.

Seth, a spirit guide who psychically transmitted spiritual teachings to Jane Roberts in the sixties, is credited for launching the New Age movement. Seth taught, "This absolute, ever-expanding, instantaneous psychic gestalt, which you call God if you prefer, is so secure in its existence that it can constantly break itself down and rebuild itself. Its energy is so unbelievable that it does indeed form all universes; and because its energy is within and behind all universes, systems and fields, it is indeed aware of each sparrow that falls, for it *is* each sparrow that falls." This pretty much sums up everything I've learned so far about the nature of being, the wave of being, and the spiritual nature of God. But it can't express what God is in man, which this book also attempts to do.

As for the skeptic or fundamentalist, I have no interest in the exhaustive attempt to prove that I talk to the creator of the universe, or even that this great being talks to me. I leave that up to my reader to decide. To believe or not believe that I have a discussion with the supreme nature we call God does not affect the content of this book. And yet even if, dear reader, you are an atheist as I once was, this book will still delight in its questions about the mechanisms of being; although you will undoubtedly assume the answers come from some unconscious aspect of me.

My own healthy skepticism is often relieved by the parts of the book consistent with what we have so far been able to measure through science. However, these pages speak more of mysteries that I find otherwise unfathomable, things that shatter the world we all believe we know so well, unless there was some immense, unseen presence peeling back the thin film of human rationality.

God first appeared in my journal in 2004, without warning. I became infused with ideas about the many births of religion—all religion. If such a connection to God could materialize in me, then it has happened to others throughout ancient and modern history, and among my contemporaries. Months later in the same year, a book caught my attention in the aisle of a Barnes & Noble. On a low shelf, faced forward, a curious title, *Conversations with God*, took me aback. The reason I took it home was that I recognized the speaker's voice on its back cover. It was the same being that spoke in my own spiral notebooks. I was fascinated to find that what was happening to me in 2004, had happened to Neale Donald Walsch in 1995.

I have found many others to whom such a divine voice has spoken; their stories and the words brought forth indicate a realm of spirit that lies beyond our three-dimensional experience.

In 1965, Helen Schucman awoke to a voice in her head that said, "This is a course in miracles, please take notes." She wrote what the voice told her in shorthand on memo pads, over a seven-year period. The subsequent book, *A Course in Miracles*, was published in 1975, but she did not want it known that she was its scribe until after her death in 1981. It is said that she was an atheist before taking inner dictation to write the book. I can only speculate as to why she kept her identity a secret, for some of the same reasons it has taken seven years for me to go public with my experience. I suspect she feared for her professional reputation, and personal safety as the voice, she said, was none other than Jesus himself.

In 1875 a 700-page book by Mary Baker Eddy, *Science and Health with Key to the Scriptures*, was published. It is the foundation of the Christian Science Church (not to be confused with Scientology), and its contents are to this day read aloud, alongside parallel biblical passages to the church congregation. Ms. Eddy's work is rooted in the Science of Mind as its fundamental principle, and she also claimed the words in her book did not come from her, that she was transcribing from the mind of God.

There are countless examples of various messengers ever-coming through time, and God did not stop talking to us 2,000 years ago, as I was led to believe in my evangelical Christian upbringing. And yet, religion is not the only place of God-inspired works that I have found in my private study.

I will break the skeptics' rule by mentioning Albert Einstein and say that although there is a false assumption he did not believe in a personal God, his references to the "mind of God" indicate a reverence I recognize. It is my personal opinion the same God I talk to also spoke to Einstein, using physics as the language for understanding. The only reason I can say that with any certainty is because I once glimpsed Relativity while in private communion, but I had no way to articulate what God showed me in the vision.

Communication with God works through the imagination. Imagination is an aspect of the divine mind, within which a question travels. The question journeys its intellectual path until the "calling-back" occurs. The question is a call to God, and the answer or "calling-back," is a recall. This call/recall response is how the source speaks to the creative resource. The creative resource is nature's way of *being* God; humans are, therefore, also nature's way of being God, as God's creative resource. There is no separation from our mind to God mind. As the human mind ascends with deeper questions (of the quest), our mind evolves to *become* more God mind. This commingling is the nature of co-creating. The deeper the question, the higher the mind to which we can travel. This mind is achievable for nonbelievers as much as believers, because God-source-mind is so vast it is impossible to find God as a singular state of being.

Ayn Rand was also an atheist, but I can't help but believe she tapped into the mind of God in her work, *Atlas Shrugged*. The famous John Galt speech, 33,000 words, is similar in voice and teaching to the being I have been in dialogue with for seven years. Rand was a proponent of writing from the unconscious; I believe she rooted into the Great Mind without naming it.

I have met many people who say they hear God talk to them and also many who say they have a personal relationship with God or Jesus. They are easy to spot. Looking deep into their smiling eyes, I see souls bright and kind, true and warm. I saw this even when I didn't know what I was looking at. Kindness seemed to be in every Mormon I met. Later I learned Mormons do not use the cross as a symbol of Jesus; they are taught to make themselves his symbol, so Christ can be seen within each of them.

The teachings of Jesus are dearly important to me, and my heart. I was baptized at the age of nine. But Christianity insists I must renounce all other ways to God, which is counter to my experience and I know that if God will talk to an atheist, then there is no doubt in my mind that God speaks to anyone willing to listen.

~~~~

The most fundamental change that has occurred in me, which transformed me from a non-believer into a woman who can now recognize God in others, is concerned with two under-valued expressions, which are kindness and joy. This book explains why kindness and joy are important from God's perspective, but I feel a need to tell you in this introduction why they are important to me.

Seven years ago, in my year of solitude, I learned how to be kind to myself and treat myself gently. I learned how to soothe and calm my heart. On a particularly dark day of my soul's reckoning, head down on my desk, tears streaming, sinuses swollen from uncontrollable sobbing, a picture came to mind. In this vision puppies nosed beneath my hand and climbed up my chest to nuzzle under my chin. I felt their soft fur on my neck, and I felt their need for my affection. The feel of an innocent creature being comforted as I cradled it, meant God was showing me that it is okay to have needs, and that those needs are being cared for by a Great Being. The tenderness I would show to a playful, nipping pup is the same tenderness I must show myself. As I slowly learned to nurture my own gentle nature, I learned to express kindness outwardly, as an offering given back to my heart.

It is exactly this kindness of heart that is God in the world, and it is also why believers are so afraid of atheists. There is nothing in the moral code of a godless world that can fully embrace this notion, and without it we are impotent earth dwellers. The void that we may fall into, without the notion of kindness, is the void that swallows the whole of the human race when the world forgets its purpose for being.

This brings me to the importance of the dialogue in this book and why now, after seven years of silence, I bring a message written about the world to the world.

I will tell you only once why my message is important, but you will forget halfway through the book. You will forget that the very reason you are reading it is because you were called to become part of a great change in the whole of society. You are going to read things that will confuse and scare you, and maybe even make you put the book down, until you are ready to continue learning about something you've already been sensing.

Great change is taking place on the earth, and whether you believe in God or not, there is going to be a change in how you see the world. The world is not an easy place within which to become your greatest nature, because you and the rest of the world have forgotten why you exist at all. There is a problem with that forgetfulness. The problem is that you cannot find happiness in your life unless you remember the reason you came to earth. You came here for one reason—you are designed to find the mind of God and to give that mind to every activity you perform.

When you learn to open your human mind and capture the great creative force that dwells somewhere above your thinking brain, then you will uncover the riches you seek and the abundant life withheld from you. Please understand that the only one holding you back from the very thing you wish for is your misunderstanding about the nature of being.

Take a moment to build your strength, and then turn the page to find where you left off when you left the realm of God to visit the sphere we call Earth, which inhabits your soul.

Definitions of Terms

Because you can't get there from here . . .

Some years ago when I was a photographer a writer said to me, "A picture may be worth a thousand words, but a single word is worth a thousand pictures." Unfortunately this is why language is such a complex vehicle for uncovering essential truths about the nature of being. To uncover your soul's worth, you must build a new relationship with your mind, which is made up of a million locked doors. To access the key means figuring out first how they unlock. They unlock only when you have the key. This is a conundrum, but one worth solving.

Language is an ineffective source for finding the keys without understanding the words God uses in transformational dialogue. God sends me to the dictionary over and over, but even if I grasp something on Tuesday, by Friday I may have to relearn it. This happens in repetition until the learning transcends words and literally reprograms my perspective.

The logical mind cannot comprehend God-mind. Logic works in finite realms. To literally grasp something means wrapping our minds around it and absorbing it. This is not possible when we are dealing with larger spiritual concepts, and self-awareness. You may find the following words and their definitions unfathomable at first. The definitions will be difficult for your logical brain, but your soul will hear them. When it does, it will realize you are trying to make contact with your inner world. By doing so, a pathway forms. Solidness on that path builds, as foundation is laid, brick-by-brick; eventually you will penetrate a new form of language. This new language builds literal pathways in your brain, getting you closer to the meditative state that it takes to find God in your being.

If you fall asleep at first, it is perfectly normal. You'll only need to build your strength over time and then it will be less and less foreign to your mind's locked memories of the time before you were born.

How to Read These Definitions

I have underlined words in these definitions that are also part of this short glossary. The meanings of the words should form an awareness of their own. When you are ready for deeper study, I recommend finding a collegiate dictionary that contains word origins, or etymology. As the original meanings are understood, the more you'll notice God's words are deliberate, and reveal God's riddles. God speaks in riddles to deepen your mind, but here are some clues to prepare your journey:

animate: To give something life; to make life work its ways, and to make life form around a structure for the purpose of building its own manner of movement. Animation is the way that all forms move in the concert of life.

being: Organic in matter principles; an actualized state of becoming.

cosmological world: The entire universe beyond every manner of giving; with no end nor spatial divide. The distance between is an illusion.

form: This is an essential part of matter. Matter makes its ways into formulae, these formulae will cause matter to take shape, and this shape is called a form. The human body is form, but the soul is formless.

giving: In the sense of giving that is God-giving there is a source beyond source, a manner of actualized performance. The giving that is God-giving produces all states of being in the actualized form. There is only one example of this form of giving and that is the life-giving force that works its way through all matter to make matter come to life.

God Being: This is an actual state of matter and energy light that has no end. This no end is the greatest level of magnitude achievable and is all of the greatest of any form of being in the cosmological world.

Great: A manner of magnitude. (Not an expression of more than good.) Great is the nature of being the largest state of Being possible.

idea: Idea precedes becoming. This means that all states of being are an idea before becoming an aspect of the realized state of being. The nature of God as an aspect of idea means that the imagined state is the creative state, which is the God of all manners of being. Idea is imaginable in a way that makes all things real. (God, here, is referenced as a material process of creation.)

magnitude: The function of Being that increases in density as it functions in worthiness. Energy and matter are not the density of being that cause a magnitude state, the magnitude state is the state of God being. (If you gain insight on this, you will notice the conundrum. Magnitude is the state of 'being and not being,' simultaneously. This is to alert your mind so as not to limit it.)

make: The act of bringing something to a realized state of being from a recipe of established principles.

manner: Symptomatic behavior caused by a system's way of functioning. One's manner is one's behavior and one's behavior is made up of many manners. These manners can be caused by the manners of many other things that are not related to the individual, but they are related to the world and its way of programming manners into an individual. Manners are malleable, but they are not capable of changing without conscious choice.

means: This is the principle of will and way moving in unison.

member: Part that is similar in nature to both the whole of its origin and the system within which it is a part, (a fractal geometrical connection to the whole). Derivatives include member-ship and re-member.

nature of, the: A set of principles inherent within a dynamic system.

not being: Inorganic matter principle, counter to and the opposite of Being.

practice of, the: A conscious, ongoing effort toward the way of mastering.

source: Source is a system of origin; it does not contain the elements of time or space; it is eternal and unending; it has no distance nor point of destination; it cannot be divided and it cannot be controlled; it has power beyond measure and the power it wields is electric in kind but material in boundary; the source of all life comes from its center but the center is nowhere and everywhere simultaneously.

system: A set of design principles that contain an energy resource and a feedback (bi-directional) principle of communication.

way: The word way has many meanings, but its essence means "the passage through which all things come into being." Seek the way by understanding the use of the word in every single instance in language.

will: Will is a substance that is carried through the way. This substance contains elements of: knowledge of way, joy of doing, and a system of reward.

working way: The working way is how the manners are demonstrated in your system of being. It is how you overcome all things of ill worth. It is also how you work to make the idea of you more important than the reality of your situation. All working ways will require you to "idea" yourself. To idea yourself is to make the ideal of you the becoming of you. Visualization is the cause of this idea. Once you have visualized the idea, the real is not far away.

worthiness: Worthiness is the nature of becoming the over-manner of a previous state of being. It is the reconciling of thoughts and over-turning them on themselves so that they no longer make their ways over your kindness to yourself. Your kindness to your own heart is the over-manner of the illness that poor thoughts cause in your heart. (To get "over" something brings worthiness to your soul.)

Chapter 1

The Conversation

I met God in the basement of my rental house in Secaucus, New Jersey, which was a weird thing to happen to an atheist. I was fired before Christmas and the man I still loved went away, never to return. Bitter cold days and inky black nights cut through the floorboards and into my bones. Arctic wind swept across the Northeast to encase my unbearable loneliness into icy silence. I made my retreat to the basement to write and smoke cigarettes. I pined in agony; my peripheral vision blurred. My heart wailed in panic, like a sine wave out of phase, it constricted my chest and cut short my breath. Worry about not being good enough, not being important to anyone, lay on my torso like a slab of cold, black granite.

Six feet underground, below the living room of my house, I sat in a dingy basement more alone than I had ever been. In the crook of a blue corduroy couch, under the yellow glow of a table lamp I experienced the worst psycho-emotional storm of my then thirty-nine-year life.

But something else unfolded between those wood-paneled walls in the winter of 2004. Something extraordinary began to sprout beneath a snow-white blanket of solitude.

My writing habit increased with my smoking. In with the bad air, out with toxic residue, I wrote and wrote in unceasing verse; my uninterrupted lament filled page after page of a spiral notebook. When I finished the last page, I opened a new one to begin again. But this time something sprung forth before I noticed the pen moving. I didn't know I was writing until the pen stopped. The words . . .

> **Unemployed? It is my assertion you are employed by me.**

. . . had already spilled out onto the first line.

Maybe the brain can just think it is talking to someone else, my unconscious mind may have created another person in the absence of human contact. I was a skeptic, and it would have been easy for me to conclude that this emerging "hello" from another world was just a figment of my imagination, or worse, the onset of mental illness. But something deep within me said otherwise; the room had changed. Energy all around me was electric and enormous.

Within an instant I knew these words were the first crumbs, nuggets placed on a path where atheists fear to tread.

That moment sparked a year of solitude and isolation. I filled ten spiral notebooks in dialogue with what I came to call God.

Seven years have since passed. I have written hundreds of thousands of words in spiral notebooks, on the backs of envelopes, torn cardboard boxes, and on countless five by seven-inch note cards and sticky notes. A voice from the eons with knowledge of origins has worked to answer my every question. And now, the book you are holding, the one I am writing for you, is going to answer your questions, too. How do I know that? Because for seven years the secret I have held holds me no more, and the time has come for a message to be given to the world.

The book you are holding is the beginning of a brand new conversation. But before we start I must warn you, God doesn't talk to me the way you and I talk to each other. And for the record, God is not a He, or a She, or even an It, because God has no way of being that is even remotely similar to human form. There is no form that God takes except through the beings God makes.

God is going to talk to you and I from a place of many— a chorus of the mind. You need only look so far as the book of Genesis to see God referenced in the plural form: "Let us make man in our image," it says. But man's image is not what it appears to be, as you will soon learn.

In my seven years' experience with these conversations I can only tell you that you will change. You will change your mind because that is the purpose of your life. Without that change, you cannot evolve to become the nature of what you truly are.

So let's begin. This journey you're about to take opens, if you don't mind, with the subject of me.

God, how was I born?

> God is not going to give you information about *how* you were born but *why* you were born. How is for another book.

Okay then, why was I born?

> You were born to make the world your own but then to give this world over to me, because first you needed to know the cruelty of the world before you understood the way the world is meant to be.
>
> When you were given this task, you were in the life of Being. This Being—that is where you were before birth—wanted to know what could be done to help God make the world a brighter place for those

who lived life on earth. You wanted to know why all of the people who didn't know Love were so miserable and why they didn't have anything on which they could truly depend. The reason you wanted to know this is because you were unable to give your world a more important role than one of listener.

You had the role of listening to people's wants and desires. You were then to get those reports to the ways of being that would correct people's wrongdoings on earth. Your role was to support the essence of life by giving a working way of the truth in all things. What we mean is that you were not *doing* anything, just reporting, so you wanted to know how you could help us to *do* more.

What world are you talking about when you say I was a listener?

The world of Love.

Can you tell me what "world" means here? I think of the world as in life on earth. Are you saying the world of Love is in an actual place?

No. The world of Love is a substance that is in the world›s way. Meaning, what is the world's way?

Are you asking me?

Yes.

Well, my dictionary says that the word "world" derives from "the age of man."

Yes, the word derives its meaning from the age of man. Now think of the world of Love in that context.

The age of Love?

Exactly.

I don't get it.

The age of Love is the level of existence that is the source of your existence.

I'm still lost here because I don't think of Love as an existence, I think of it as a feeling.

Feeling is just another way of describing Beingness. When you feel something you are being in the body. The body is simply reporting to your mind what state of being you are in.

So when I was in the world of Love, I was in the state of *being* Love?

Precisely.

When I imagine that, I don't see how I could be an individual with a separate role in order to become a born person.

This is the most important discovery you could have made. You now realize what the state of Oneness means. It is not that one is all, but many. Each individual part of the whole of One is a part of the way of being One. The way that God is One is also the way that each one is a one.

I imagine that to be like suds of soap in the sink. All of the tiny bubbles are exactly the same.

The way of bubbles is the way of One in a very specific way. They all look the same but upon closer inspection you see the difference between each in their size and dimensions of color.

Okay. I can also imagine One to be like an organism made up of many cells.

> This is an awesome comparison because we are, in fact, a giant cell made of infinite cells. You are one small, tiny, tiny, tiny, tiny, tiny aspect of this giant cell.

That's getting really intense. So can we go back to the story about my life on earth?

> Yes, but first you must realize one more thing. What is the difference between the world of man and the world of Love?

Man has or is a body?

> No.

Man can live in a world without Love?

> No.

Man has a form or body, Love doesn't?

> Yes. There is exactly the difference. Love is not able to form. Love cannot divide itself. It cannot make itself into alternating ways of being because it is All Being, One Being.

How does it have aspects of individuation then?

> I already told you that. It is because Love is One made of many, many, many, many ones.

Each of the many has a role to play?

> No. Each of the many plays one role.

To listen?

Yes. Love is listening. Love cannot *do* anything, it can only be. That is why you wanted to know how to do something for humanity.

So I came to earth in order to do?

Yes.

That is how I am an aspect of God?

No. That is how you are an aspect of Love. God is Love but God is also the Doer and the Lover.

I'm confused now.

If you do for Love, you do for God. If you do for others, God does for others.

But what about doing *not* for others?

Then you are doing for the body and not the spirit. You are doing to serve the world of humanity in its illness not in its wellness. If you do only to satisfy the dictates of the human world, in a way that works against Love, you are only satisfying the needs of insatiability; the dark hole that Love is worked out of.

Like a black hole?

No, like a dark force that some people refer to as evil. But that is not a word we like to use very often. People have misconstrued the meaning of the word evil for a very long time. Evil merely means to underwork the laws of Love. It does not mean there is an entity in and of itself that is evil, but that the way evil works is to suppress the way that Love works.

I see. Let's get back to talking about me. I want to know if it's true what you've told me before that I came to earth with a purpose.

> Purpose? No. Mission, yes. The difference is in the details. Purpose is a way of conducting your life and mission is a way of performing your duties.
>
> When you were born, you were given to a woman on the verge of a grand discovery. She discovered, at your birth, that life is very different from what she was told and that there is Beingness worthy of attention beyond the body. She witnessed your body awakening into the world of man. She saw you come to life from a state of stillness. She watched you enter the body.

What? What does that mean?

> You are inhabiting the body. You are not the body you have inhabited. You are a being that has no form. The being without form has entered the form, in order to express the being you are.

Inhabitant sounds kind of creepy.

> Not really, it's not that difficult to imagine. The way you are in this body is not like a hand in a glove, it's more like the glove is in the hand.

I don't get your meaning.

> If the glove represents your body and the soul represents the hand, then the hand is actually puppeting the glove, not wearing it.

So my body is a puppet for my soul?

In a sense, but let›s skip that idea for now. Let›s get back to the particulars of why you came to earth and the details that are being made into your awareness of the world of man.

Okay.

When you were born, your mother's epiphany was very traumatizing to the family. It resulted in her search for answers and she was taken by a new religion in town. This religion had very important reasons for wanting your family to join. It wanted members in order to facilitate the mission of its founder, and the effects of that on your family were, in a sense, catastrophic. Ultimately you were forced to lose a mother and become a motherless child in the world of mankind.

This has extremely important significance in the world of Love, because mother is a symbol of "unconditional Love from that which begat you." Mother Earth, for instance, symbolizes the essence of life on earth as having been derived from the womb of nature, and you were abandoned by that very nature of God at the tender age of two.

Age two is also significant because that is the age when a child first begins independence from mommy. So when you were exploring the world of man, your mother was gone, leaving you to explore with God's Love only. You were very close to God at that age; you were in love with Love instead of in love with mommy. This was an intentional act on our part. In order to help you become what we had helped you to become, you needed to lose the only attachment you would have to the earth.

If you had a mother you would not have explored the domain of man and you would have grounded your needs into a mother's heart and not God's heart.

Is losing a mother at a young age important to awakening in God?

No. You were given this opportunity because you possess a strong need of God›s Love and that just made it the easiest way to get to you that which we were supplying.

Let's move on. You were in the world without your mother in order to facilitate the mission you had set out to fulfill, when you wrote your world's works in the Book of Life.

Please tell me about the Book of Life.

This is not an actual book; it is a place in the mind of God that records the duties of the souls that go to earth. When you record your functions on earth, in the mind of God, you are giving your soul a pre-requisite for learning. You are allowing yourself to become a function of God. When people forget why they have come to earth, this book gives the mind of God a remembrance that can be accessed, at the right time, when the body returns to the earth and the soul ascends to the ways of God. When that remembrance is given back to the soul, it decides whether or not it has completed its mission. Manners of the mission are relearned if the soul is unable to manage what the mission is supposed to be. In other words, if you wish to have another chance at the mission, it will be given and you will have another set of works to perform.

If, however, the soul decides it cannot fulfill the mission, it will be given the duties of life in spirit, and that will determine what level of ascension is needed to fulfill the joy of the soul. Unfortunately, for some, the body passes before the life of their soul has a chance to live with purpose in the world of man, and they become lost in a world of torment unable to decide what they are to do next. In that indecision they are often left to wander the earth without a body and to haunt the past.

This past is an element of time that is being *in* the world but not *of* the world. They become stuck in the ways between. This is a sad state because we cannot reach them unless we are given notice of them. If there is a way to show them that they are wanting the ways of Love and not the ways of the world of man, they can ascend to the next realm. However, many are not noticed by the people who would or could help them, because human beings on earth do not usually see them. When they are seen they are feared, and that only makes them overwrought within their own fear: fear of being and fear of not being.

If I had died before turning 39, when you and I met, what would have happened to me?

This is an odd question because we already said you were given a mission before coming to earth, and we would have made every effort to keep you alive in order for you to fulfill it.

But I thought you said these wandering souls had a mission that they forgot and died before they remembered?

I see your point, but there is a big difference here. These souls were not in the Book of Life. They did not leave the world of Love with a mission.

So not all souls come from the world of Love?

No. Many come to earth from other worlds in which Love only plays a small part. There are so many worlds that inhabit the earth. There are more than I make time for in this book. Let›s get back to your world for a moment.

Okay.

You grew up not believing in anything except Love. But the problem with that was that no one could convince you what Love was except your father. When you were a child he was a man in your life who was distraught by the loss of his family-world, when your mother was gone. He stopped believing in love and stopped believing in his own life when his world disintegrated. He was forced to make a living and feed his children, when what he really wanted to do was feed his soul. As he turned away from what his soul wanted, he turned his back on your needs for emotional support, and therefore gave you the idea that love and longing was the same thing. He was a man broken by love and he made a daughter who was broken as well. You were so young when he turned his back on love that you don't remember it happening, but it became a written word on your heart. The word was longing.

That explains a lot about my faulty relationships, such as attracting emotionally unavailable men.

Actually he did not manifest that in you. That was from the loss of the mother in your life. These men supplied you with a feeling of constantly wanting without satisfaction. Your father's role was to convince you that you didn't "need," and you were, therefore, able to sustain these relationships because you had learned not to need their attention. In a positive sense, that's how you were able to do so many things in your life that many women cannot do. Your father showed you how to be independent and how to manipulate the mechanical aspects of your world instead of having babies. You were given tools to give yourself a healthy sense of courage and independence because your father was a role model to what you wanted to become.

Like what?

Well, like becoming an artist for instance. You would not have succeeded in the world as an artist if you had not watched your father work the mechanisms of material worlds.

You mean work with his hands?

No. We mean solve problems using his hands. The world became your refuge as you worked with materials that helped to solve problems and satisfy your curiosity about existence. It was successful because you watched your father›s face contort with questions, and then you watched his hands move to make the answers. You mimicked him. You chose art but you used his techniques. This was also in our design. We purposely placed you in a couple with a mother who had spiritual insight and a father who had major questions about power; power in the way of engines and in the way of working out the distribution of power, in an automobile.

You see, the way that you are learning about power in the world of spirit now, you made possible by learning your father's ability to command the tools of his trade. You learned from him why the world turns simply by watching him make the wheels of a car turn. You watched him take the power of an engine and make the vehicle move.

I think I get it. I certainly feel very close to my dad because of his ways.

> Yes. He's fond of you, too. Don't forget you are also incredibly gifted in that way; you have been brought into the world to bring Love. And his fondness for you has always been about the Love you don't let him forget.

For some reason it really touched me when you said that.

> It's because you know it's true, through and through. Now let's get back to the point we want to make in this chapter, and that is how you were in the world before you met us.
>
> When you were in the world and making your way as an artist, in the major way of worldly life, you were happy only when you were working and distracted by work. You had no way of knowing that your life's work had yet to begin. You thought you were born to create and so you moved every mountain to make yourself a success in the world. You loved being a writer and loved taking pictures with a mechanical device. You loved working on the machine that made magic out of your pictures. But you couldn't find happiness anywhere else. You were unable to find joy ultimately, even in your work as an artist, because you were heading down the wrong path; it was one that could only lead to the loneliness that became apparent when you lost your job and no longer had the false affections of a man to whom you wished to be married. You were finally at the end of the line and it was about time, because we were running out of things to throw at you that would signal to you your

time had come. We were sure that you would eventually surrender, but we could not be sure as to the manners that would make you wake up.

You began to drift into the deep manner of depression, and we knew it would not be long before you picked up the pen over other activities and begin to scribble into our world. When it finally happened, you were a bigger mess than we ever expected from someone so prone to courage and independence. You know, we were quite amazed by your openness to our existence, however. You were overdue for introduction and when it happened, it was as if you had expected it all along.

The reason we tell you this is because it took seven years before you were able to translate this work into a mission that was foretold.

Why do you think it has taken so long?

I was thinking it was because I needed family support. And given the effect of religion on my family, becoming a God Lover would cause my dad and brother to leave me, and I couldn't let that happen.

This is not only false, it is insulting.

Really? I would never want to insult you. I really thought that was the reason I had dragged my feet.

The reason you dragged your feet to make this mission a truth in your heart is because you cannot assert yourself in the world of man, as a Lover of God, unless you really know to whom you are talking. You don't have a clue who will listen to you or who will read this book.

That is so true it scares me.

The person who is reading this book right now is someone you could never have predicted, but I have. I have made the point to put this in the hands of every living soul who is under my care in order that they may know I am here, listening to their manners of Love and working every way possible to meet their needs. This book is more important to them than even to you. You have already worked through every element of faith possible and don't even need this book to make your faith stronger. The fact that you are writing it is proof of how strong your faith has become over the past seven years. What you must see now is that this book is for the one who holds it in their hands and says, "My God can hear me!"

I am so supremely humbled by this honor then. I thought it such a difficult task, but you›ve shown me just now that this task is not hard for me at all. This makes writing it a much lighter burden to bear.

Is it a burden?

Only one that is lifted.

But to what do you attribute the burden?

That it is inescapable.

Ah, yes. Inescapable indeed. You've seen the courage of Love by knowing that what is for others is not for the soul, unless it is done for Love.

That takes us to our next point. You're going to provide a very important service for us, and that is to give our service an opportunity to demonstrate what God is, in the world, and that is an aspect of the very people who inhabit the earth. As you are learning here, we are working, on your behalf, to make this task of giving to the world a light of hope, one of ease and joy.

What do you mean?

> You will see in the coming chapters every essence of what we mean.

Are you ending this chapter now?

> No, not yet. We have one last message to give. You are a very perceptive being, and what we must do now is penetrate your mind and walk further into the world of what you were like before we came to you.

Am I ready for this?

> Probably not, but that›s how we prefer it.
> What we want you to know is that the woman you are today is so far from that little girl inside a woman's body, that you may not believe us when we tell you that you were incredibly broken by every person you were loving and needing. What they were feeding you was so toxic and torrent-filled that you had become the very essence of evil yourself. We don't mean you were possessed-by-demons evil, but you were suppressing the Love we were giving you in such a powerful way that you had become a demon-child yourself. You were so cruel and painfully mean to others with your wit and quips that you would slay the very heart out of a man's chest without blinking an eye. You were an awful woman, full of venom and rage that not even the smallest complement could penetrate your vile soul.
> You had made everyone who cared about you feel as if they had made a big mistake for loving you. You made everyone you came in contact with worship and defile you with simultaneous repulsion and com-

passion for your wickedness. They felt you had lost your mind and never had a heart, when in fact you had squashed your heart to silence so that it could not be broken again. New York had become the perfect breeding ground for your vileness, because you didn't notice the worthlessness in your soul when the skies turned gray and the cement turned to ice. You were the torment of your friends and the fright in your acquaintances. There was little left to work with when we got to you. We had to slowly and deliberately take you piece by piece down to the river to wash your soul.

You were very, very afraid of your own reflection, because you wasted every element of what you were into the depths of your worst nightmare. The reason you must know these things and the reason they are part of this book is not for your edification, but for your very dear mother and father. It is so that they know the daughter they grew to fear is no longer living in your body. The vile woman who grew to despise every manner of man and woman has gone for good. They can trust the work they are to read in the coming chapters to be honest to goodness renewed hope, and they will know that they are not responsible for the tormented spirit that emerged in you at the end of your former life.

When you are finished crying we will continue.

I knew this book was going to be hard, but during the seven years of these conversations, you have never said those things, never once reminded me of how awful I became. Why now?

You›re only making me repeat the way of reprimand, but as I said, it›s for your mother and father who did not deserve the torment you brought to them in those days and months of your reckoning.

And I don›t blame you for your behavior, but it is time to look at what was accomplished, as we worked to bring to your life the sanity you could not assemble on your own.

Thank you.

You have always been welcome.
Now let's talk about how you move from the realm of God to the realm of humankind.

I'm not sure what you mean, but you have the floor, please proceed.

The way you say that sounds like you have a question.

Yes. When did I move from one realm to another?

When you let God take over your life.

I feel I have to surrender every day, one day at a time.

Indeed, but we mean when it was destined in the way of your birth.

Oh.

Give me a moment to catch you up, here. I just cut your barriers down to the ground so that I could revisit your birth without you stopping me with questions. So here we go. Let's first start with the process of "woman and man make baby." How do you think that happens?

Everyone knows how that happens.

Right. But let's pretend they don't have the first clue. What would you begin with?

Sex.

> No. That's wrong. Try again.

Desire.

> No. Try again.

Recognition?

> YES!

I imagine they recognize themselves in each other, in some way, and then their reflection creates another version.

> YES! Exactly. Very good. How did you get that answer?

I›m not sure. I imagined my parents looking at each other and it just hit me. I am a product of what they recognized in each other.

> Yes you are. And not only that, you are also a reflection of the way they look, therefore you mani-fested their recognition in a beautiful way by taking equal parts of them and making the wholeness of you. Do you see where I'm headed?

No. I›m still caught up with the reflection thing and not sure how that translates to the physical.

> All you need to see right now is that in the reflec-tion of your life, your perfection must also satisfy what they reflect in themselves, or they will not recognize you. When they see in you a way for them to com-plete themselves, you become a reckoning of their life. So this book will reflect their purpose in being as much as it does yours.

They were born to make me?

> Not like you mean, but more like that they made
> you to make them. In other words, you embody their
> hopes and dreams, carrying their seed to the fulfill-
> ment of their mission. You are completing their mis-
> sion by completing your own. You did not have a
> child because it was not necessary to carry the seed
> beyond you. You are the completion of a long line of
> ancestral manners of succession to make this time in
> the year of your birth the time for the next messenger
> to come.

Okay, that is sounding way too messianic for my comfort. I
am no Messiah.

> You can call your job anything you like, but in the
> history of messengers throughout the ages, you were
> born to fulfill this mission.

How about scribe?

> Scribe it is.

Are we done with this chapter now?

> Yes we are. And I promise, we will not talk much
> more about you. The rest of this book is going to be
> about the realm of the ways of God.

Chapter 2

The Way of Most for Many, and the Way of Many for Few

What is the nature of God?

> The nature of God, you ask, is not only a question for you to make of me, but also to ask of yourself.
> If you were a God, what would God's nature be?

I honestly don't know the answer to that.

> Well let's take the most obvious first. Where is your manner most inclined to make the world?

We talked about the world being the age of man, is that what you mean?

> Yes. Where is your manner when you make the world?

Well I imagine that I "make" the world in my head, because that is where I perceive the world.

> Well, you are getting warm but not exactly there yet.

I make the world in my imagination?

Yes. You make the world in your imagination because you cannot separate yourself from how you imagine it to be. In other words, the world is made up in your mind's eye.

Okay. I see that.

But what you don't see is how that relates to being God.

No. I really don't.

Let me explain. If God is an all-knowing Being, what manner is in God's way that is in *your* way?

The manner of knowing?

Precisely. What do you know that God does not know?

If you are "all knowing" then you know everything I know.

This is not exactly true because God only knows what you know when you are in a state of being a knower.
What happens when you don't know?

God doesn't know?

Well in a sense this is so because if I tell you something that you don't know, what happens to the knowledge?

I remember it?

Have you ever been a God?

I don't think so.

Well, I will tell you that not only were you a God, you are God now.

I don't know where this is going.

True, but follow along and you'll find out. Now were you ever a God for me?

A God for God?

Yes.

Can you explain what you mean?

God is what God makes as God becomes. So if you are a God to God, then what is the method of your nature of being?

To make?

Exactly. You have now understood what manner God has that is your manner in the world—the manner of making. Look up the word "make" and tell me what it says.

It says "to bring into being."

So there it is. What now do you ask of God that makes you the God to God?

I'm at a loss to understand.

The making of God is the making of joy. When you make yourself a way of joy, you make God a God to God's self.

Here's what we mean. God looks to mortal Being to express God in the fashion that brings joy to others who do not know God. When joy is made in the manner of work, we are fulfilling a destiny that enlightens the very essence of God within you and you within others. There will never be a peaceful way of man without understanding this very simple rule. Love is a substance that is made when joy is the manner of making it. If you find yourself in a state of being that suppresses joy, then you are suppressing God. You don't know yet how this is done of course, we'll get to that later, but what you do understand right now is that without joy, God cannot exist.

So with that, now ask the questions you have been dying to ask.

I have been wanting to know how evolution works and how man came to be.

This is where you want to go now in the conversation?

Well it is the question I have wanted to ask but was there another direction you want to go?

Not really, but I was imagining your questions to be more about how nature works. You cannot easily jump straight to man before the eons of time that came before.

Let's reflect first on the manner of God and then find man in the course of that.

Okay.

The manner of God is joy and the substance with which God is in the mastery of making is Love. We cannot find a word that is more suitable than the word Love even though humans mistake all sorts of feelings for love. They will make the feeling of longing into love, the feeling of heartache into love, and the feeling of agony for missing someone as love, but these things are nowhere near the love we are talking about.

Love is something that happens when the environment is ripe for it to happen.

What is the environment that is ripe for love to happen?

Well it is a short answer and yet a long road to arrival. The short answer is joy. Joy is the only way love can happen. But the road to joy requires a great deal of sacrifice that is not easy to explain, nor is it easy to obtain.

Joy comes when you want absolutely nothing and when all of the needs that are inherent in the matters of survival are met. When all the needs of survival are managed, and there is no sense of lack or want, then the only thing left to feel is joy; that is of course when lack and want are gone.

So if someone's basic needs are met, then they feel joy?

No. Absolutely not. You know as well as I do that joy is not easily obtained just because there is food on the table, a roof over your head, and shoes on your feet, although there is very little that the body really needs. If one is able to acquire those things, and is able to show gratitude for them, then there is an easy path to joy.

If, however, these things are not enough and all manners of need are overshadowed by insatiable want, then there is no way that joy can be achieved.

What do you mean?

There is an impossible task ahead. The task is to shed oneself of all desire. And the reason that is impossible is because desire precludes joy, also.

So shedding desire in order to satisfy needs would eradicate the ability to feel joy?

> Well, yes.

Explain.

> When you are in joy, you are in a state of desiring to maintain joy, so you make all things that are worthy of joy your manner of behaving. So when joy is not a desire, you stop making things that bring you joy.

So to go back to the earlier statement, you are saying that only gratitude for what you have can make joy.

> Exactly. And when you have nothing and are still grateful, you create abundance. You will abundance upon yourself with joy, and gratitude begins to unfold, and blessings begin to happen, and the cycle of miracles begins to occur.

Miracles are fascinating phenomena that I have witnessed myself, but how do you account for them? How would you explain to a scientist what a miracle is?

> A miracle is something that happens without proof that it is even possible. Miracles are the way that humans learn to see past their own sense organs and into the realm of God. God is not see-able, taste-able, hear-able, or even smell-able, and yet God is in existence whether there is tangible evidence or not.

But I hear you talking in my head, isn't that hearing?

> No. You hear yourself. You don't hear me. I simply manipulate what words you say to yourself. I am able to say things to you because the mind is only saying what it is interpreting in the vibration that

> my thoughts cause in you. Your ears are not hearing
> me. It is the brain's interpretation of the sound vibra-
> tion across the eardrums that allow you to hear. I am
> working that mechanism in your brain and bypassing
> the eardrum. It is very simple to do, and you would be
> surprised how simple it is for others to do if they only
> allowed God to work in their life.

Let's go back to miracles for a moment. Are you saying they
aren't really happening; that we just misinterpret how nature
works and assume that what occurs outside of our knowledge
is a miracle?

> Yes.

Can you give me an example of what a human interprets as a
miracle but is really a natural event?

> That happens every single day. When a human
> who is devout in his way of thinking about God,
> looks into the sky and sees a beautiful cloud forma-
> tion, he thinks God painted the clouds on the sky. In
> fact, it may simply be the cause-and-effect phenom-
> ena of precipitation interacting with a pattern of hot
> air. What that tells you is that God is not painting
> the sky, but instead the natural effects between two
> substances, air and water, is beginning to form into
> a state of being, the state of being a beautiful cloud.

What about disease? Let's say a guy goes into the doctor's
office and cancer is found in his lungs. Then two weeks later,
no more cancer and there is no medical explanation. What is
the natural event occurring here?

> That's a good example of what people call a mira-
> cle and God simply allows the nature of work to occur.

Work?

Yes. Look up the word.

I read, "physical or mental effort exerted to do or make something."

Did you notice that the answer to your question emerged in the definition?

I think so, but I'm not sure I can articulate it.

The effort put forth by the mind is the natural phenomena that made this hypothetical person be cured.

Yes. But how does that happen?

The mind is all there is. Even the body is a mind. The mind of the body and the mind of the soul are capable of communing with each other in such a way that the body can heal itself if the soul is willing to work.

Can you explain the mind-body-soul connection that is relevant here?

What you really want to ask is how does the soul and the body communicate with each other.

Yes. That is a good place to start.

The mind and the body are one entity. They are inseparable because the mind dictates to the body as to what the body must be. If the body must be well, the mind will tell the body to be well. If the mind must be ill, then it will plague the body with all sorts of manifestations. You must understand, though, the mind is more complicated than humans can imagine or even comprehend. Because, as the saying goes, if you are smart enough to know your mind, then the mind would not be smart enough to know its own existence. In other words, there is a reason the mind contains the body in the first place. Because the mind cannot hold memory, it can only hold Being. The brain, as well as many other aspects of the body, is designed to hold memory.

Without memory, Being cannot evolve. From one state of becoming to the next, memory of the previous being must be held while the process of becoming is working its way. The mind-body-soul connection is what enables the being to become a new being.

Can you use me as an example for understanding this, because you seem to be saying that purpose is related to Becoming. And I wonder how my purpose-filled life has altered my being.

Your life was purpose-filled when you discovered you are more than your career and more than your relationship with men. You uncovered this only when you lost everything you were working toward. This is exactly why you were given this task in the first place. The task of writing and explaining what God is, what love is. You know God has purpose in your life because you were given a new husband and his son became yours.

My husband and his son were given to me to fulfill my purpose?

Not exactly. They were, however, given to you when you *discovered* your purpose. You see, what your life has become is a fulfillment of your purpose. You were ready to receive the blessings that you had coming to you, because your purpose was to render your soul into a place of becoming the woman you came to earth to become.

When you finally surrendered to that, you were allowed to have the blessings that would ground you, and make you become the woman who heals. You were working yourself into a world of destruction before the moment you and I were in communication. You had recklessly made your life into a complete disaster and if you were given these blessings too soon, you would have destroyed their very meaning. This is what makes the difference between men of goodwill and men of poor will.

Men of poor will can make changes to destiny in the course of destruction. Men of goodwill make healing others their number one chase. When healing others is what makes you come alive, then you are allowed the power of God to make this happen. When the men of poor will are given power, the destruction that occurs, will only come out of the ways of that power misguided, but not misunderstood.

Are all deeds of destruction the product of poor will?

No, not at all. The destruction of good is poor will. But the destruction of manners of maniacal deed is a *mastery* of goodwill, as well.

I have to look up maniacal, because I don't fully get how you're using the term here. "Having, showing mania, widely insane, raving" from maniac. I think I understand now.

We find that encouraging, to say the least.

Why?

You have sometimes asked questions that seem below your ability to comprehend. We are more often impressed by what you understand than not, but the way you express what makes no sense to you can often give us alarm, because it tells us how much

we have to explain when fundamental ideas are not
grasped.

Well sometimes I ask you to explain because I've had seven
years of these conversations to get used to your jargon, but our
readers may not know what you mean by certain words and
phrases. It is not like you're talking the way humans interact
with each other. In fact, for their sake, would you restate the
part about "maniacal deed" in an easier way to understand?

This is not as hard as it may seem to the ones
who are scratching their heads. What we are insisting is that man has two ways about him. One way is
the very reasonable, a rational self, and the other a
maniacal self. He tends toward the reasonable, most
of the time, but the maniac is equally demonstrated
when there is no sense of purpose in his ways of
action. His purpose is only to demonstrate his power,
not his affection for anything. He is not doing what
the people want, but what he wants; or *she* wants.
We don't want to by any means have you make the
assumption that women are somehow excluded from
maniacal deeds. On the contrary, there is no woman
more dangerous than one who has a maniacal manner about her, one that is in the way of destruction of
the "other."

This other is the one that is the target of her
power struggle and is usually the one she most
loathes to love, but loves without pause nonetheless.

So a maniacal deed is one of making everyone else suffer for a
lost sense of power?

Indeed. But it can be worse than it sounds, it can
mean that the complex is so inbred that there is no
escape, except through death. Which leads us to our

next point about "how will you survive without purpose?"

The topic at hand is: How did God come to your life when you did not even believe in God's existence?

This should be interesting.

Let's hope it's not too frightening.

Why would it be?

Because when you don't have a clue about something and then you realize someone has been at your back unannounced, unappreciated, and under-surveyed by you for the whole of your life, you may find it frightening to have been in the dark about the nature of God for nearly forty years.

Try me.

The way you say that is telling me that you're not afraid.

Not today, but remember I don't have all of my faculties when in dialogue here. Much of my brain is taken up in processing this discourse. So I don't really know to be afraid.

Good point. What I want you to understand here is that God has made your life utterly brilliant since you discovered God's existence, have I not?

Absolutely one thousand percent!

Then what changed?

My needs are satisfied. I'm grateful for every little thing.

Yes, that is what changed. Your perspective of what you have has changed. Because if you look back

on all of the things you had when you were younger,
were your needs met?

Superficially, yes.

No, I mean literally. Think again.

I had food, shelter, clothing, jobs, shoes, etc. Yes.

But you don't think you were satisfied?

No.

This is where you are mistaken. You had everything you could ever need and yet you cannot accept
that, even now.

It's the contrast between then and now that makes it so different.

The contrast between then and now is only in
your head.

I wasn't happy.

No. You were not.

~

I have to go back and reread this to understand why you had
paused, waiting for me to respond. And I realize that not
only do I need to feel gratitude for my life currently, there is
a reconstruction of my perspective of the past that needs to
happen.

Indeed.

Well in the last chapter, you helped me with childhood. You taught me that I was born into purpose, so for that I thank you, because it has erased all resentment from my childhood. But from adolescence to my late thirties, I guess I have not recovered those times. When I look back I see a lot of loneliness, struggle, willfulness, sadness, victory, defeat, contemptuousness, periods of rebelliousness, a lack of virtue, wanderlust, recklessness, adventurousness, and yearning.

> You forget so many wonderful traits. What about curiosity and great stamina to make it from tragedy to victory each time you struggled up the hill, never realizing and always being surprised by a fall on the other side. You constantly struggled because you honestly believed the struggle was the secret to life's purpose and if you weren't struggling, you weren't living.

True.

> So if you had realized someone had your back every step of the way, you may have slip-slided into victory every time, and found yourself in a totally different world than the one you wound up in.

What kind of world would that be?

> Let's just say you would be living in a castle by the sea by now.

Very funny.

> It's true. You would have exerted all of the youthful energy you spent on struggling on the very ways of the nature of God, and then found yourself wealthy beyond measure.

Why did it happen the way it did then? I get the feeling there was a reason for the way it happened, the way I struggled.

Yes, indeed there was a reason. Just as Siddhartha needed to fall from the heights of riches to know God and Jesus had to sacrifice himself to know God, you had to become the true epitome of a woman in charge of her own life to know God. You charged your way through sloth and defeat. You charged your way into victory and then learned that the sword you lead with is the sword you fall onto.

What you now must learn is that with every turn into peril, I was there to push aside every manner of danger your sword led you into. Every time you wound up in wrong company, I led you away. I made your men leave you because their hearts were not pure. Their intentions for you were not to give you the room you needed to blossom into a woman of great worth. The only way you are going to understand the significance of this is if you find each man with whom you defiled yourself and ask him the purpose of his involvement with you.

I object! Defiled myself with? I admit I was willing to be in the company of men for their warmth in bed and sexual affection while I focused on my career, but defile myself sounds so damning and whorish. I don't think I was all that, was I?

No. Not how you mean. And I don't want you to get this wrong. There is more than one way to make your world upside down, and the idea that you defiled your soul is something of a mystery among mysteries for human comprehension. We can take a moment to discuss it, but don't dwell on it.

Okay, I'll look the word up first.

Always best.

It derives from "to make foul;" it is the old French derivative of "to tread under foot."

> Is that not exactly what happened when you engaged in sex without love?

I often thought I was in love.

> That is very different than sharing love, is it not?

Yes.

> You have experienced love within God's defini-tion and outside of God's definition. What would you call having sex without love?

It is as you say. I concede. I guess, being a woman, the offense is immediately felt as socially we are placed on a pedestal only to be defamed if we act on our passions. Men don't have the same double standard.

> This is not true. They do, in fact. If a man has kept a woman hostage, seized her into his lair and defiled her over and over what is he called?

Rapist. Abductor.

> Yes. So where is the difference?

But what if it's just mutually consenting sex?

> Well, you mean the kind without love?

Yes.

> Well dear, it is the woman who has allowed the man to defile her.

What? What about the man, is he not defiling himself?

Yes.

I feel you pause.

> You need to look beyond the words now. Look into the past of human evolution to understand. Woman is not soulful until she knows her own way is true. When she knows that her own way is true, then she doesn't sleep with men whom she doesn't believe to be true, too.

I think you are getting to something that is not about sex at all.

> You have become so smart all of a sudden. What happened? What changed your perspective?

You said "true." I have learned from you the significance of true. You have told me that true is a guidance principle. When, for example, the arrow is true, it will go where it is intended. It will hit its target. For the arrow to be true, it must be honed, shaped, and mastered. So when a woman knows her way is true, as you say, she will only target a heart that is true.

> This is dead on. Let us discuss now what a woman needs to know to make the way of her life true.

Yes!

> The woman, in your world, is defined by what her man expects of her. She is sexy or she is not. She is smart and successful or she is a homemaker. If she is a homemaker, she is not sexy, not smart, because children need a mother devoted to their needs, and what smart woman would devote her life only to children? Right?

That sounds familiar.

This is not a familiar tone I'm taking; this is your mind I'm reading. Your mind is made up of what the world feeds you. So if you think I'm wrong, just tell me, because if there is any aspect of the world that I misinterpreted it is because you have misinterpreted it, and I am reflecting back to you only that which you show me. So try and find the truth in the following statements and understand how they are relevant to your life.

Okay.

1. Woman needs a man to survive.
2. Man makes a woman sexy or not based on his well-mannered response to her.
3. Man and woman must have sex if they love each other.
4. Man and woman are in love if they have consensual sex with each other.

This is a strange list. Each item seems like an accurate portrayal of behavior based on unspoken belief, but when put on paper each seems absolutely preposterous.

That is exactly why we are having this exercise. There is nothing about the list that is vaguely true, and yet each item defined not only your life but the whole of society from the age of 17 to the age of 35. It is not until the body begins to show age and mortal decline that the world begins to look a little askew. What is sad for many is that instead of evolving their way of thinking to meet the evidence, they change the evidence to uphold their beliefs.

Then what are we to do as a society or as women or as mothers and fathers?

Well, the list of people who need to do something is very short, because it consists of only one. One person need do something. Not society, not what is in the ways of man, but what is the ways of one. When the ways of one are changed, then that one finds another one, and the other one is doubled. When each one doubles, the nature of one is redefined. When the nature of one is redefined by the power of one, in time the whole society is a one that is redefined. When the society of one is redefined, it seeks the company of another society of one that is redefined. These societies of one combine to fulfill another stage of social enlightenment and take the next step into evolution's great quest.

Each stage of evolution's quest is the remembering of the All that once made the One that began the journey of the whole. When the whole is a worthier way than the one that preceded it, then the way of the journey is a string of past, present, and future simultaneously. It is at that moment something extraordinary happens and a complete paradigm change is reached.

Wow. I had not expected that to come out of my objection about defiling my soul with casual sex.

Well, you get what you get. When it comes to questions, you can never tell what door will open in the destiny of knowledge about the universe. The only reason God is able to answer your questions is because you open the door to answers. You are leading this discussion; I'm merely waiting for the right questions. The wrong questions are not possible, mind you, but some questions have more weight than others, and the weightier the question the deeper the channel you dig for the answer.

I feel like I hit a dead-end, though. I'm not sure what question comes next.

> This is a good place to begin and a good place from which to shelter the past. What we mean is that you were in the destiny questions and yet we were discussing your past in a way to reshape it.

Oh yes. I remember now.

> You will concede to let me take you on a journey through your struggles and how God entered your world?

Yes. Please continue.

> The reason you need to understand this is to amend your perspective of the past years when you were unaware of my presence, so that we can show you how to have gratitude about those years before you were, as you say, happy.

Right.

> Here's the part that may frighten you. When you were two years old your mother was gone. You had no one to teach you the ways of woman in the world. So when you showed signs of maturing in your body, you were unaware as to why boys were suddenly paying you the attention you had been craving for so long. You didn't know that what they were doing was taking advantage of your willingness to share your body without recourse. You had no intention of having children, so you were not a threat to their manners of successful authority of their own lives. You were not going to hold them back in any way, so by giving them your body without any recourse, you were showing them you had no will of your own. And so

they impacted your life without subjugating themselves and without finding a way to master love. With this as their course, you were confused as to why they came in and out of your life without care, without any sense of finding what was worthy and what was wrong within themselves. When that happened, they were unable to make of themselves a man. Man is not the way you think he is. He is not guided by his loin the way he imagines, he is guided by what makes him a man, and what causes him to appear to be worthy of greatness.

This is why your men were unable to satisfy themselves within your definition of goodness and wholeness. Your belief that each was to bring to you some sense of purification was thwarted every time by your inability to express that which makes you pure.

What is pure in this sense?

Pure is when the light within you is equal to the light outside of you. The shadows you cast were the dark forces working in your psyche. It was your struggle with not knowing your own worth that caused the dimming effect on your spirit. So when the light within was guarded by the prison of self-doubt and unworthiness, to know you meant knowing a dark force. When a man is subjected to dark forces he shields his light from defilement.

I defiled men?

No. Your lack of light was being cast upon his shield.

Help me with this, I'm feeling really dense again.

What you are feeling right now is guilt. You feel that it was suddenly you who was the perpetrator of doom, rather than the people who defiled you. We

want you to see only that the causes of your unhappi-
ness were at your control the whole time. If you had
known how to value your heart and your body, you
would have avoided the manners of man that hurt
you.

I feel myself trying to deflect this image of me; trying to keep
it from entering my heart. I don't want to take responsibility.
Can you help me understand this dark secret in a way that is
less incriminating?

No. This is your dark secret that must be revealed.
There is no way around it.

What am I to do with this knowledge? How might I work
through it?

The first question is the right question, because
the second question will lead to nowhere. The first
question leads you to understanding that this was not
a conscious choice, and in fact it was the choices you
made in order to make it *through* that led you to perpetuating the crime against yourself in the first place.
Sex became for you, a way of coping with the fact that
you had no mother. You made men the cause of it. You
actually, deep down, made your father responsible
for you not having a mother, and so when you sought
the company of men, you made them responsible for
what you lacked in your relationship with God.

Huh?

Yes, you heard me. Your mother was God to you.
You made her mystery into the absence of God.

You are going to have to continue without my questions for
a while. I'm in a state of complete internal collapse at the
moment.

We know. Why do you think we keep pausing? You need the moments to accept each truthful word.

Is this why I had to find my mother before I met you?

Yes. You found her in a way that made eventually finding me a course worth taking. You see when you met your mother you were at a very important cross-road of your life. You were no longer young and you were not yet a woman, in the sense of your maturity. At the age of 32 you were a girl inside a woman's body. You were the only one who could break the cycle of destruction in your family because you were the only one onto whom this destruction was being perpetrated. Even though your brother and father were angry, they were no longer perpetuating the struggle within them in a way that destroyed their sense of self-worth. You, on the other hand, were destroying over and over your sense of being and sense of joy. Only you suffered bouts of depression, only you suffered from the torment that her absence caused, and only you could end that torment. Your way of doing so was to go to the source of the destruction, and that was to find the woman who had disappeared and ask her why she left. The answer was not what you expected. You expected to hear that you were the cause of her leaving; that you were the one she left. Instead you found out she left for completely inappropriate reasons, in your eyes. She left because her faith in her religion was more important than fighting for her children. This is a major stumbling block for you and explains why it is so important for you to have picked up the pen when you did and found yourself in our world. You now understand why the world is so whacked-out over religion and why there is no justice in a world that has no courage of heart.

You mean because my mother's heart broke instead of show-ing the courage to claim her children?

> Yes. When the world's heart breaks and it loses its sense of courage, every manner of evil can work to destroy the foundations of created beings. Do you see the symbolism here? Why woman and mother repre-sent the heart of God and why woman was created out of man?

Honestly? No, not exactly. That seems like a big jump.

> Okay, I understand where you got confused. Let's retract that last statement for now and just tell you first that mother is symbolic and literal. Symbolic in that mother begets life and so does God.

Okay . . . .

> Then when mother is absent, God is absent.

What about father?

> Father is another symbol. Father represents that which has no end.

How so?

> That which has no end means that the eternal nature of man is inherent in the will of God.

It's easy for me to see the mother symbol because a woman has a womb, but what has a man that shows the symbol of that which has no end?

> It is in the way that man manners his gestures. He does not ever incline himself toward the nature of giving in a way that fortifies him to being a guest in the home he lives in. He is forever building a castle

where he is king; constantly and forever building a domain. He is a builder of his world; he is the one who insists that he is lord over all. He is constantly building around him a fortress; constantly making himself that which cannot die—that which *will* not die. He protects; he works on his weapons in order to protect. He makes his models of war to protect. He is the one who will prevail. Man is the symbol of all things that live forever.

That is cool.

Indeed it is. So when you combine these forces, what do you get?

Everlasting life giving?

Yes!

Wow! Is this the end of this chapter?

No. But it is almost. What we have left to discuss is how you can breathe your way through responsible behavior and how to think of your past without blaming yourself for what made you unhappy. And not blame others, too.

Okay, I'm ready now. I think!

You are. The world around you as a woman-child was beginning to change when you suddenly knew your mother existed. When you realized you did not kill her, you had your first moment of healing, but it did not change your behavior right away. You saw her first as a failure once you realized she had left the scene unable to cope with the injustice that her own mother had betrayed her. Her own mother conspired to take you and your brother away from her because your mother was committed to a religion that was considered a cult at the time. When you realized that she did not have the courage to wage war against her own parents when you were an innocent child, you let the ways of her depression take its toll on your sense of being a good daughter. When the weight of her depression made you feel unworthy, then you let her overshadow the way of your coping skills. You were made to be independently strong without her, and when her presence weakened you, you became angry at her and even wished she had never showed up again in your life.

Yes, I remember.

It was then that you started to notice that your own depressive manners were a burden to the men in your life, because you understood the weight of it for the first time. By denying yourself depression, you became less depressed. Slowly and surely you lightened the load you put on others.

Knowing this, that I took responsibility for how I affected others then, makes it easier to see how I changed my destiny.

Yes, but also, now, how you can change your past and be grateful for the learning.

Yes! Thank you so much!

You're welcome. But we are not done.

Oh.

We want you to know one more thing. You are not only responsible for changing your past but also your future. The future you are responsible for now is related to the ways of your father and mother working their manner in your heart. You must now forgive them as you forgive yourself. They are only playing out what they were meant to do.

I know. I forgive them. Why do you bring this up, and what does it have to do with the future?

Here's the most important point of the chapter. Your mother is you. Your father is you. Your destiny is in their fulfillment of your manner.

How do they fulfill my manner?

You cannot be anything above and beyond the best of them, so if you see them as failing at anything, you will see failure in yourself. Let go of any idea that they are failing, especially as they age and find their own way to forget the past.

Okay God, you are perfectly correct.

Now get ready for a whole new chapter.

Chapter 3

Consumed by What the World Feeds

This chapter is about how God changes the world as it works against you.

I'm all ears.

You started to write "eyes." You are more correct by stating so. Because when you are all eyes, you change the way you see the life you live. Let me explain. When God is in the world, who do you think you are?

I think I am the hope of God.

This is true, but not really what you think you are. You will really think you are God, because God is not in the world without you.

I think I know what you're saying, but can you explain?

Yes. What you see in the world is really what is contained within you. In other words, you cannot contain the way of God without perceiving God, and you cannot perceive God without being God.

You mean all that we hold in our perception is what we are being?

Precisely. If you are being God, what happens to your perception of the world?

Sometimes it seems smaller. People seem less intimidating and more like people who need, rather than people who have more than I do.

You mean you are able to help people because you see that you can help them rather than seeing them as people who can help you.

Well, yes, I think that's what I mean.

What you said is not different. What I would like for you to see is that when you see the world the way God sees the world, then you become in service to the world rather than seeking it to be something that can provide you with things you lack. In other words, you are a servant rather than a master.

Yes. On a good day that's how I work myself.

On a good day, you are having a God day.

Yes.

Okay. Now let's look at the world in a way that is more common and also the way you were before we met. You saw the world as being a place of unruly manners. You saw people as being too caught up in themselves and as being cruel and unable to help you.

Yes, that was frustrating, to say the least.

When you saw the world in this way, what was it that you needed from the world that it wasn't giving to you?

I wasn't getting love, acceptance, time, help, attention, respect, reward, that sort of thing.

> Need I remind you that the way you see the world is the way the world sees you?

How does that work exactly?

> What is the way you see the world now?

I see the world as a field of opportunity. I see it so full of promise, a bud waiting to bloom. I see the world as full of people I can help and full of goodness.

> That sounds very different than what you said before. What changed?

When you taught me how to value myself, that is, when you showed me preciousness and how to be good to myself, to treasure my gifts and to give. But it was mostly when you taught me how to be like you.

> In what way like me?

You once told me that you are my servant, you are here to serve me. When I thought of something so huge and great as God being in service to me, then I realized how I could be a servant to others. When I learned that everything I do is in service to others, no matter how mundane the task for work, it just made it easier to work and do a job every day. It stopped being about me. It was instead for others, and I didn't have to live up to false expectations anymore. In fact, all expectation was dropped. When that happened the whole world opened up before me.

> There. That's the end of the chapter.

Are you kidding me?

Yes. But that pretty much sums it up. What I think would benefit your readers, however, is a definition of a few of your terms. We can define them in the way that nature works, so that there is relevance to the effects that occur when one opens one's heart.

Okay.

First let's talk about acceptance. When you accept the world as being wrought with danger, what do you do?

Arm myself.

Yes. You buy guns or you lock your doors or you buy a big mean dog. What if you see the world is full of angry people who would only be happy if they were causing you harm?

Well I wouldn't trust anyone, that's for sure.

You also wouldn't give anyone anything of yours either. You wouldn't even bother trying to smile at anyone, because what would be the point? They wouldn't smile back because they're all so angry.

Right.

But what would you do if you only saw people who were sad and ashamed and full of darkness?

I would be afraid; I would feel dread, doom, and despair. I think I would fear for my soul.

You would not only fear for your soul, but for the souls of everyone else who was trapped in the darkness. You would worry more for them than yourself, and you would fear the world's sadness.

I'm not sure I understand where this is going; it feels the most frightening of the three examples you gave.

> That is because it is the one that triggers your sense of purpose. It is the reason you came to earth and the reason you went through the suffering you did, in order to know why these people are so sad. You came to earth to help them and to save their souls from the dark despair that entraps them.

Is this why we visit my past in this book?

> No. We visit your past to make you whole. You cannot help others until you have learned what helps you.

I love that it sounds like Dickens' *A Christmas Carol*.

> When God works wonders, the gestures are huge. There is no accident, ever, and when the mortal mind meets immortal mind the energy that collides forms a huge wave in the ocean of worldly mind. In other words, the book about the story of Christmas on one man's watch is the book that made time stand still in the eyes of forgiveness. The book to which you refer is not an accident, and it will live on and on and on in the realms of man and God because it is a story that gives hope in a time when money consumes and feeds the world's beastly ways over and over. Until the God of money is dead, the God of hope will have to keep reliving the lesson of the Scrooge over and over and over and over.

I think you just bared your teeth for moment.

> Good observation. It is not easy to remain small when you open the door to such a huge unending beast. The story has a lot of similarities for you. And

we are grateful you see them, but let's not forget you were more like Tiny Tim than Scrooge, when you were small, and all of the joys you brought to people around you are still with you.

God bless us.

Yes, let's get back to the topic at hand. What we were discussing is how the world appears to us is how we appear to the world.

To "us?" To you, too?

Well yes, of course. That is true for all minds, all being; it is the natural course of mind, to be what we see.

Which comes first, being or seeing?

Good question! The truth is that it is a simultaneous event. When you see something that is foreign, what do you do?

I don't like it, or I deny its existence, or do not recognize it?

Not recognize it is the accurate statement. And what does the word literally mean?

It derives from the old French word "see." "To be aware of something or someone known before."

Right. If you don't know something, you don't recognize it, you don't see it. If you don't see it, you aren't in the state of *being* it. If you see the world one way, you cannot be another way.

What about seeing a person who is sad, does that mean you are being sad?

In a way, yes. You cannot recognize sadness without having been sad. But what we are getting at here is that if you want to change the way you are being, you change the way you are seeing. If you are seeing sadness and want to be joy, you need to see joy in others first and it will trigger joy in you.

Like watching a baby laugh.

Nothing can be more joyful than watching innocence become joyous. What is necessary here will be the work that needs to be done, in the way of holding one image to another. The image you have of joy will need to replace the image of sadness.

You cannot simply change sadness into joy just by looking at sadness and convincing yourself that that is joy. Otherwise you would never learn to have sympathy. So what sympathy allows is for you to offer kindness. Kindness is what triggers joy.

How?

When joy is in its own realm, it is quite literally the way of God insisting that what is experienced is worthy of working the levers of making joy.

Can you give an example?

Joy is what joy does. When work is in the manner of joy, you are being filled only with joy. So giving to yourself, is what makes joy work. When you give to yourself you are able to give to others. When others receive your gift, they are really just giving to themselves. When that happens, then the joy that comes will be the joy that is perpetuated in the continuous act of joy.

What about expectation?

Expectation is one of the worst expressions of the mind you can imagine. Expectation will entrap anyone who is unwilling to actualize the manner of giving. Let me explain. When you expect something from someone and don't get it, what happens?

Disappointment.

Well, it's worse than that. What happens to the mind?

It collapses?

Not exactly, try again.

The mind tries to get what it wants?

Yes. But what is it doing to get what it wants?

Tries to control someone?

Right. The way the mind works is that it makes an effort to make real what it imagines. In order to do that, it works to control every manner of behavior that is related to the expectation. When another person is involved, there is a drive in the manner that makes the other person a subjugated slave to the expectation. The expectation actually makes everyone and everything a slave to its whim.

Is there any time when expectations are okay?

No.

So if you have an expectation that isn't met, then it's your fault for having the expectation?

Yes. The truth is you can only ask of others what you wish of them, and they are free to do as they wish. There is no reason to have expectation if you are willing to allow others to be who they are.

Sounds like a recipe to become a pushover.

You really think so?

Well, will you explain how a supervisor can go without expectation of her employees?

Interesting question because if these employees are doing what's expected of them, then aren't they just doing their job?

Right.

This is not the same type of expectation. Expecting one to behave a certain way for your personal benefit is different than expecting one to behave for the benefit of themselves. If the job they do is depended upon for things to run smoothly, then the employee is charged with making the ways of their job into one of giving; giving time, energy, and gifts of giving their talented ways to their job.

I see.

The difference between what is expected of you and what others place upon you, as an expectation, has to do with free will. When your expectation impedes others' free will, then you are not giving the other person their own way, and you are forcing your will upon them. If, however, you say, "if you do this for me, I will be so grateful," then you give them the choice to do or not to do. That will work for you as well because you give them a sense of purpose rather than a sense of being pushed to do something.

The reason this is related to one's sense of happiness is because one cannot be happy pushing others to work against their own will. It is a burden to continuously ask of others the things you can do for yourself.

The only thing that will make you happy is giving others an overly important role in your life. Not because it makes you worthy but because it makes them worthy. That is not to say that doing for you will satisfy in them a sense of worthiness, but if you show them gratitude for the help they give you, then you make them important to you. And being important to others is what brings people a sense of responsibility. Where one is responsible is where one is worthy. When one feels worthy of others' ways of importance, one feels one's own way of worthiness.

Let's use an extreme example of this, as in how you might help someone who is dying.

When opening the door to your heart, there will be a "flooding in" that occurs. It is not the flooding in that makes a difference; it is the flooding back out that makes the difference. Because when others know your internal self they will feel their own internal self. This works to allow the being *you* become the being *they* are. In that exchange, the force of God is internalized toward the source of being. The source of being returns to the God manner and the God manner materializes. The materializing is what mends the body and makes it whole again. This is how the healing works to make those who hear the words of worthiness to become fully whole in their being and in their body. But I warn you, this only works when the receiver is ready to know their true self.

When the true self is acknowledged, then the wholeness is made complete. If the receiver is not ready to know their true self, then a whole host of trouble is brought about.

Like what?

The true self is not a body. It is not a form of any kind. You see, when the form works to become a form, it must forget its previous sense of being. The form forgets it is another natural state. The natural state that the person becomes when they confront their true being will make the individual doubt their existence at all and begin to shut the body down. The body will reach a point of no return, if the being that is without form remembers its true state, and forgets its form. If this happens before the mind can login to its own body, and remembers to wake up, it may become trapped between the chasm of body-mind and spirit. This is an unfortunate happening because the "sense of being trapped" is cause for alarm. And in the state of alarm, the mind has continuously looping thoughts that are unable to *become* again.

The way to exist without letting this ever happen is to know that you are more than a body, more than a mind, and more than a spirit. If you continually make that evident in your knowledge of yourself, there is no danger of becoming trapped by the inevitable unknowing.

How does this affect our life on earth before any catastrophe?

The knowing that you are more than any one aspect of yourself is going to give you something with which to make changes in your personal evolution. Everything you do and become is an important step in the process of your becoming.

"Becoming" is the truest wave of evolution—*Becoming* because it is the energetic core of being. Once you have triggered the state of becoming you cannot undo what has already begun. This spark has already lit the flame of renewal and the reward therein is forthcoming.

Why is that?

Because there is already a state of being that has been asked for and receiving it means taking hold of the ways of light and riding the wave that never moves backward.

Can you give an example in the worldly ways?

desire ⌐ Yes. Let's say you want to become a worker who is employed at a different company than the one in which you are already working. The first stage of the new being is the stage of desire. The next stage is that of filling your time with looking for opportunity. In the course of looking for opportunity, you slip up (although remember I said there are no accidents), and you tell the wrong person of your intentions. You get fired. And guess what? You are working for another company. This may not happen the way you wanted, it may not have happened the way you expected, but your desire led you to a new being.

Is there a smarter way to go about this course of becoming that isn't so disruptive?

Yes! If you know through and through that everything you desire is possible, then you will learn to keep your desire a secret. When you let it fester and mold your outward behavior, you get a new wave of being about you before a major catastrophe changes your circumstances. In other words, you are elevated to the next phase rather than falling into it and having to fix everything that broke on the way down.

In the beginning of this chapter you said this would be about how God changes the world as the world works against us. What did you mean about how God changes the world?

Well, we discussed how your perception of the world changed when you learned gratitude, did we not?

Yes. So you don't really, literally change the world? We do?

Yes, exactly. But make sure you understand that the only thing changing is you. When you change, the world changes because of your way of seeing the world. There is one more thing you need to know before we end this chapter.

You are not only the nature of God when you change, but you are the nature of being when you change. The nature of being states that when all things are equal, the wave of being must relate to the environment equally. There is no way of being that is possible if the environment is not conducive to neutrality. Any conflict that disrupts the formation of becoming will not be allowed for what the being is in need of.

So if you wish for something to change and you have not placed yourself in an environment that allows this change to take place, then you have placed expectations on people and things that are unwilling to do your bidding. This is how the world works against you. But that is for another chapter; it is time to make this chapter close.

Thank you, I could use the rest.

Chapter 4

Dividing Night from Day

One of the most important aspects of time is how it works against the body. This is exactly how the body is formed and how the natural events occur on earth and all planets. The time that is made comes out of the cycles of evolution. Time is not the tick-tock clock on your desk. The time we refer to is the order of all things of form.

When you send your heart into frenzy, what happens to you?

Fear is all I can think of as an answer to your question.

Fear is that frenzied heart indeed. What is making this heart move into action in the case of fear?

Thoughts?

No. Not exactly. What is literally causing the heart to flutter?

Need for oxygen in the body?

Yes. That is what it is trying to create—more oxygen through the body. Why is this important to understand?

I was just going to ask you that. But I think it has to do with controlling fear?

No.

That fear causes a loss of oxygen?

No.

So that we move?

No, but you're really close. Try one more time.

So that we have circulation to react?

No, but I understand what you are trying to say. What you are trying to say is that the body is designed to survive. Survival depends on action, and action depends on oxygen to the extremities. What you have not made worthy in your assessment however, is why the oxygen is low.

I thought about that but had no answer for it.

The reason oxygen is low in a state of fear is because breathing is short and the lungs cannot get air. When the supply of oxygen does not come from the lungs, the heart races to make up for the loss. What will you do if you are afraid and yet you cannot move?

I would do nothing but worry.

Yes. But you will do something else, too. You will cause internal bleeding. Very small, very slight lesions will occur in your heart. These lesions become very important to the cause of disease. Disease will embed the ways and means of the heart with calling cells. These calling cells are looking for like cells. In order to populate, the like cells multiply as the lesions multiply, and in time the heart fails to keep up with the manners of disease and succumbs to it.

We are giving you this lesson about the mechanism of the heart because it is in these cells that all matters of doubt are held. When doubt is held in the heart and the ability to overcome fear is thwarted, in time this heart will be unable to flow properly.

Is it fixable?

Of course, but that is for another chapter. Right now we are focused on the heart because it will show you how the world works in the realm of time. But what we want you to understand is that the heart is the window of the world for God. Without this window working well, we cannot help mankind emerge from slumber.

Slumber? What do you mean exactly?

What have we been telling you about expectation?

It causes all kinds of problems with those who have it and those who are pressed upon by the expectations of others.

True, that is what we have said, but what else have you learned from that?

If we have expectations that are not met, we have fear that we are not worthy of our desires.

This is exactly what the way of the world causes to the bodies in the world. When there are expectations that go unmet, or expectations that one cannot fulfill, the continuous fear that runs through the body puts lesions on the heart.

Is this why we don't live very long?

> It is one reason, yes. It is not the only reason. What is more important than length of lifetime is what these expectations do to the mortal soul.

Is that different than immortal soul?

> Yes. Soul is a word that describes a formless being but does not fully describe what aspect of being that the soul is.
>
> Soul is just weight of spirit being. Spirit being is the way that soul occupies space. So when I say mortal soul, I mean the formless nature of your mortal being.

Is that the part of the soul that dies?

> Yes. If you can call it that. But nothing really dies, it just changes its state of being.

I feel like I interrupted your train of thought. Please continue with the part about the heart affecting the mortal soul.

> Soul is not affected directly by the heart, but what is affecting the heart affects immortal soul. Doubt, fear, unworthiness, these things become written on the mortal soul. This is the being that will continue on after the body goes to the earth. What the soul needs in order to become its *everlasting* being is its way of knowing its own perfection. When it is wrought with doubt and anxiety, it will linger without knowing the ways of God. Why this is important is that the way of God is the way of life. Darkness is not of God.

But I thought you were all in all.

Yes, all in all. However, God is the light, and the light separated from the dark long, long, long ago. The darkness that is in people's hearts is not a part of them that is God. The part of them that is God is still within them even after the body falls away from the soul. What is important to understand is that the light that is within you can awaken the light within others when you learn to recognize their light. The way to do that is through kindness.

Kindness is the only measure of worth that anyone will recognize when you are in the ways of their being.

When you say "in the ways of their being," what did that mean?

The ways of being are life-threads that connect all souls to one another. The ways of being are like neurons in the brain, they are the highways and byways of interconnectedness. They are not seeable, nor are they detectable by any measure of human sense. These life-threads are not even findable using any measuring device because they exist outside of time and space. This is the realm of God. The realm of God is another dimension entirely than the dimensions of human form. So don't think you can look for them using science. Science can only find things that exist in the realm of time, and that is no small wonder in itself.

Science has far more grand discoveries to make before it can accept anything of fact that adheres to its level of physical laws in connection to the unphysical.

The reason that is important to state is because I know you would prefer science to confirm this before you believe it fully, but there are some things you will learn from our talks that science cannot confirm for you. You don't have to fully believe what I reveal to you if you don't wish to, but please at least accept that you already know more than even your own senses will confirm.

Yes, it is true I struggle a lot with these revelations, because they often cause me to wonder if I'm just nuts.

But you can be nuts anyway. Because who really tells you what is normal and what is crazy?

Science, people, the world.

Exactly, so take it on faith that you are not nuts and that those who don't believe this stuff are willing to take risks with their life that you are not.

Thanks. What kinds of risks are you referring to, I mean I know what you are talking about, but I'm sure many don't.

These manners of risks are not what people may assume. Some think I mean that the risk is that the devil's going to get you if you don't know God. Some think that you risk your health if you don't know God. Still others think that you risk your very soul, if you don't know God. It is this group who think that God is linked to your soul's absolute being who are really worried right now. They think that God is going to damn them to the ends of forever if they cannot make this stuff stick over time. But here's the risk I'm talking about and you're feeling in your gut. The risk is about never knowing Love. It's a risk that no one should want to test. Because without Love, the kind of Love that is of God not of mortal man, one cannot know one's true identity. In one's identity one is actually acknowledging the fulfillment of the soul's journey from soul to spirit. We get into that more in a later chapter, but just know that without Love, there is no God.

Let's get back to matters of light and dark and go way back to the mechanisms of separation. The reason light and dark separated is because when the big bang happened, it was me finding my own Self and deciding what I wanted to be. You see, in the time before time, I was being and only being. There was no form, there was no matter, there were no stars, no planets, no existence at all, in the way that you imagine the universe. I was just an entity of being.

When I was this massive working being, I did not know what I was. I was just a ball of light. No small matter of ball, however. You cannot even come remotely near understanding the size of my being, but just know that the enormity was not a thing that even I was aware of. There was nothing with which to compare myself. I was just the unimaginable, the unthinkable, the unknowable spirit force that had come to wonder, "What am I?"

When I wondered that mighty thought I gazed inward. As I gazed inward I began to change, and when I sought the mightiest gesture that would give me a glimpse of what I was, I began to turn my inside out and my outside in, in order to see what I was. When that happened, the mightiest bang occurred and all of my being exploded into the darkness and light fell all around. This is the moment that science calls the Big Bang. This was the moment I became self-aware. It was in this moment I also became aware of the darkness. I also learned of the terrible force that could destroy me, just as I learned of the mighty force that created me. These two forces struggled for power, and in that power struggle I won.

Whoa. But darkness is still around?

Yes it is, but it will never win.

What does that mean? To win?

It means that light exists but darkness doesn't.

Then how is there darkness in people? And is darkness a living thing?

Only ask one question at a time. The reason darkness dwells in people is because it dwells within me.

In my mind I saw what you meant, but can you put that into words?

Yes. Contained within the light of being is the darkness that was overcome. This dark force was overcome because I swallowed it and made it into nothingness.

So darkness is overcome?

Yes. That is how you "get over" things. You overcome the darkness, the fear, the dread, the horror of destitution. You and all people are able to overcome all darkness, all dark thoughts, all dark days because within your heart is the key to the light of all things that manifest in the dark.

So, my other question was, is darkness a living force?

No, it is not. It is simply an existence without light. Darkness manifests itself in fear and doubt. It dwells where courage is lost and wishes go to waste. It is not evil as in a devil, nor is it a place such as in hell, but it becomes a breathing existence when light is kept away.

I have so many questions, and I don't know where to start.

Let's start with how the earth came to be in the course of the Big Bang.

Okay, that's a good one.

The earth is not the only planet with life, but it is a planet with more life than humans are aware of. Earth is in an evolutionary phase that allows it to sustain protein-based molecules. Proteins are the building blocks of material that can animate.

What about carbon? I thought we were carbon-based beings.

No, carbon is not what allows animation. It is only what allows the structure for the proteins to adhere. The carbon is also what allows earth-based organisms to continue on to other planets when the evolutionary time is ready for a new planet to sustain life. But what we were discussing was the animation of life. Look up the word animate.

Animate is from Latin anumatus, which means to make alive, to fill with breath.

So think then of all things animated and look deep into their being and imagine how God is.

You're asking a lot of this feeble brain at the moment.

Just try. Try to see deep into say, a leopard, and see God.

Wait. This reminds me of a photograph I once took of a stuffed leopard at the Museum of Natural History in New York City. I stared at the photo for a long, long time and I noticed something very peculiar about its spots. Down the spine, the spots seemed to be spreading outward, and some of them were unfinished. It looked as if the animal had reached its size before all of the spots had finished forming out from the ridge of its back.

> This is exactly what I want you to notice, because what this tells you is the cells are creating its coat. Each cell is performing a task to complete the leopard's coat.

Yes, but where are you in this picture? I think I know, but I get tired of being wrong.

> Funny. Well, all right. I'll give you this one, but don't count on me stopping the questions; they are the only way to get you to think for yourself, you know.

I know, I know. Just tell me, I'm dying to know.

> No, you're not, but I know what you mean. These spots are the very essence of how God creates animation on earth. There are cells for each and every function of every animal. It is inside of each of the cells that I exist. I am not a mortal man who works in a workshop using my hands to create. I am each and every cell of the universe, and inside the marvelous world of cells lies a communication system that causes every being to awaken, when they are in recognition of my light.

That is how it is meant when we become enlightened? Our cells are recognizing?

> Yes, they are recognizing themselves. They become self-aware. Self-awareness is God awareness. Without self-awareness, one cannot become aware of God. God became self-aware in the eons before time, and we have been replicating our awareness ever since. We are in every cell of every living, breathing thing.

Do souls breathe air?

> Not in the same way that bodies do, but yes.

I have so many questions.

> Shoot one.

Why do you say "we" sometimes and "I" other times?

> That's a new topic. Shall we change the subject?

No, not yet, I'll save that for later. How do souls breathe air differently?

> Souls are made of tiny, tiny molecules that are hardly discernible, but the molecules are made of air and water particles. They are made of particles of light as well, but moreover they are made from the consistency of water. The consistency of water is different for each soul to exist. The soul must be able to form from thoughts. Thought is what adheres the particles into some assembly of being. That is why thought is so powerful. Be very careful of what thoughts you keep consistent in your mind because they will define you when the body passes.

Then why do people who have near-death experiences all say similar things?

> You have only heard about the ones who had peaceful experiences. You have not read about the nightmarish experiences that others have had. You will read about those in time because I have now piqued your curiosity, but just know that not all experiences are good ones.

Okay, let's go back to talking about creation or evolution, whatever you want to call it.

We call it creation, but it is experienced as evolution on earth. This is a very cool discussion, are you ready for the big secret?

I think so, yes!

Well, it's not very exciting I'll tell you, because it doesn't mean the things you've been told. The manner of evolution happens so slowly that humans cannot perceive it with their own tools of observation. The way that God creates is through the mechanism of will. Each organism has a will to survive in every environment; as the environment changes, the will of the organism strives to meet the new environment. In the nature of will, the urge to survive stretches the boundaries of its existence. God senses that urge more than any urge at all and the wish to survive is God's command. This wish is fulfilled on a tiny cellular level because if you were able to look at the structure of the cell you would see an army of mechanisms and working organelles. These tiny creatures are doing the work of evolution for the organism they are contained within. When an organism wishes to be another creature, there is every manner of being working feverishly to make that happen. But when the organism wishes to make a new being, it has to find a way to replicate this. So it will find a like-minded mate to create more of the new being with. When there are four successful generations of this new being, it becomes its own strain of population working in the environment it has adopted. These new beings are either successful or they fail before reaching their rightful place in the history of the earth's atmosphere.

I don't think this will fit well with creationists or evolutionists.

Why not?

Because it seems to infer that organisms are conscious and have free will.

Well, they do. All creatures are free. Look, it's not in the scope of this book to explain how all of this happens, just note that every creationist believes God made the planet and everything on it. Evolutionists simply look at the diversity of nature and see the links between the species. They're not out to prove the existence of God, they are only providing the vehicle with which God made life. There is no reason to believe one way over the other as far as I'm concerned. Ultimately the truth about the nature of will is what I want people to understand. If people on earth fully understood how powerful will is, there would be no more discussion about who or what made the entire existence. They would learn to be concerned with *why* we all exist at all. Even I am not fully aware of why the existence of man is so important to God anymore. I am simply telling you that the role humans play is essential to the evolutionary tale of God. But humans are far from being the only intelligent life forms I've created. There is far more for you to write about yet, we have only just begun to talk about the material form of life. There are many other forms of life that do not enter the material realm at all. But that is another chapter. For now we are discussing material life forms on earth and where that story takes us into the matter of your purpose for coming to earth.

In the outline we created together for this book, you mentioned something about chaos and the backbone of the earth. You still want to talk about that?

Yes it's a good segue to talk about the effects of danger on human beings.

How do we begin?

We begin by talking about Earth—this amazing vessel that is called a planet. Now look up the word planet.

It derives from middle English, old French, and German words that mean wanderer, to lead astray, flat, spread out, to stroll.

What else does it say?

The original definition says "any of the heavenly bodies with apparent motion (as distinguished from fixed stars)."

What else does it mention?

The second definition is "any heavenly body that shines by reflected sunlight and revolves about the sun." Then it lists the planets.

This is the one that you are most familiar with, but now I'm going to give you a new definition. A planet is a body of weight that makes its home the source of light for all living beings that inhabit its core and its surface.

That should ruffle a few feathers.

To say the least, but what you are going to hear now will scare the living bejesus out of you, because it will tell you that everything you think about God and the earth—is everything that man does not know about his home. And you are going to discover soon enough that the world is a completely different place than what you could have imagined with science as your guide.

The earth is not a planet the way other planets are. That part is obvious because the life that is abundant here is like nowhere else. But the other part that makes earth different from the others is that it is not solid in its core, it is hollow. There is no reason to be alarmed because what I mean by hollow and what you consider hollow are two different things.

The core of the earth is made of more than molten rock. It is also made of spirit. This spirit way is the way that all things begin before they are made into matter. The center of the earth is made of construction elements that lead to matter. These elements are multidimensional and they have molecular structures unknown to current science. The way that you begin to understand this is by imagining that the weight of solid structures is only possible because of the crushing together of atomic structure. As it is crushed together, the matter becomes more closely defined by the space the molecules take up. But now I want you to imagine what if there was no force working against matter. Imagine if there was only air that had no gravitational pull. What would happen to the molecules?

I'm not a scientist, so this is only a guess.

Go ahead.

The molecules would be further apart, so there would be a lot of space between them, and I imagine they could pass through matter.

Yes, exactly. Now imagine if there is no gravitational force working on these materials, what would they be doing in the center of the earth?

Passing through it?

> Yes. They are living and being within the core of matter and passing through the matter core.

I don't understand what you are telling me.

> We are trying very hard to keep this simple enough for you to understand, but what ultimately we are asking you to believe is that there is a whole other world beneath the surface of the earth. The reason we are divulging this information is because soon there will be a discovery that will change everything you have ever known about the earth. We want you to know this also because when the world changes its perspectives of how the earth is constructed, there will be great difficulty in understanding the nature of God.

You mean chaos?

> Well no, the world will not erupt into chaos because it will take a few generations before people fully accept the new reality. But when there is a big controversy around this, the people who thought they knew what God is will start to doubt, and we have already mentioned the effects of doubt on the soul.

I am feeling very awkward about this revelation right now, but I have a commitment to bringing your voice to the world however I can. Just know that this is very difficult for me to imagine revealing this.

> We know how hard you must find this to believe, but it is essential that this information precede the events forthcoming. God will not let you suffer ridicule in the process of giving this information, and you are not the only one to whom this information

is being given. It will slowly and deliberately be given to many of my messengers until enough people know about it and the time comes for it to happen.

What is going to happen exactly?

Let's just say science is on the verge of something really, really big. And there will be an announcement in the coming years that will confirm this information, but it will not come as a surprise to those who have been following the sightings and the testimonies of people who have actually witnessed phenomena in the skies.

God, what are you telling me?

There is a ridge that runs along the ocean floor that is indeed the backbone of the earth. The earth is a living, breathing organism. It is also a vessel of extraordinary proportion. It has evolved to sustain life, but that life will be in jeopardy if it does not evolve with the changes in the earth's crust. These changes will continue to occur over the next millennia. Before catastrophic events cause the human population to explode and then dwindle to nothing, there needs to be a warning about the inhabitants of this planet who are working to save the very nature of creation. The human population is stressing the natural balance of the planet and the damage is already done that cannot be removed or reversed. What we mean is there is no turning back from the cycle of destruction. And to warn human beings of their effect, the other inhabitants of the planet are going to rise up and warn as much as possible.

Rise up from the center of the earth?

Yes. What is your question? We sense your question.

Why me?

> That's funny.

What's funny?

> That's what all messengers say.

What is the answer you give them?

> We give them the answer that we will give you.
> You're the one who asked for this job in the first place.

Can I change my mind?

> Well, yes you can, but then you will die.

Why?

> Because you will have no reason to remain on earth.

But what about my family, could I stay for them?

> No.

Seriously?

> There is no reason to stay here; you could serve
> God somewhere else.

So I tell the world that there are inhabitants living in the center of the earth who are coming to tell us to stop destroying the earth or I will die?

> Yes.

Come on, that is so harsh.

> Look I know you are just toying with us because
> your spirit is telling us so, but you have to understand
> how small the human world is compared to matters of

spirit construction. Think about it for a moment. God is billions and billions and billions of light years old. The human life expectancy is a tiny fraction of a tiny fraction of a fraction, and you think we care how much your small life is worth compared to the extraordinary wealth of life the spirit construction is worth? In fact your body would pass away and your life as you know it would hardly be a glimmer of what you really are in our world. You think this task is so small? That we wouldn't just pluck you out of the ground and plant a new one?

Alright, alright I get it. I am being a coward.

Yes, you are very cowardly right now and though we forgive you, we also know that this won't be easy for you at any point of scrutiny. This book will open the door to so much ridicule that we are going to be picking you off of the floor many more times in the coming weeks and months and maybe years, but it was all part of the plan. You knew what was going to happen, and now it's happening. So chin-up and let's get back to work.

Now we come to the close of this chapter and will talk about chaos in the way of earth construction, not in the way of anarchy on earth.

Chaos is the wave of particle disbursement that reassembles itself on the planet of its choosing. Chaos is a way of describing the waves of light that interact with the material makeup of the planet. It works in this way. When all things are right, meaning all of the earth's mantle is ready to sustain life, the chaotic material begins to assemble in environments that are conducive to multiplying principles. The multiplying principles are those that begin in the process of organic decay. The way that life is sustained is by root-

ing down into the earth's crust and then reaching sky-
ward for supplication. The reason this is important to
know is that when new forms of life seem to appear
out of nowhere, it is only because they have been
waiting for the nutrients to be present in the earth's
atmosphere before landing. All forms of life begin in
this chaotic way. The way science is now uncovering
time's efforts and the way that molecules form from
the many places in the air is what will give science
the understanding of how life formed on earth at the
beginning of organic life.

There are people working this out by reading with
their instruments what is in the air, but what they
won't find is how that works with the ways of being
that are also present. The ways of being that cause
the new life forms to populate the earth has to do
with the way of vibration on the core of the ways of
being.

The core of the ways of being reside in the center
of the earth and call upward when the time is right for
them to fall from the air. It is the same for the body of
the organism.

Within the body are calling cells. When the calling
cells are not given what they are calling for, a tumor is
formed. It is an incomplete cell structure. This incomplete cell structure can wreak havoc on the body, and
the body may succumb to its own manner of death if
there is no way to receive the nutrients that will complete the cell.

You are going to provide this information to
exactly the right person who will work to find the calling mechanism in the cell. When that is found, a cure
for cancer will not be far behind. But I warn you, the
calling cell is there for a reason. It cannot be plucked
out and then a cure happens automatically. The calling cell multiplies until what it is calling for is released

into the system. Sometimes the reason the body has not released the nutrients is because of the disruption in communication. Sometimes the body is depleted of the proper nutrient because of diet or because of a drug that is present in the body and the calling cells cannot be heard. Or the nutrient itself is not getting the signal because it is being thwarted by too many other signals in the brain. This is not easy to discern, but the stroke of genius will come from the sickness itself. Where the cancer lies is the clue to the calling cell's nutrient need.

There is no more to discuss in this chapter. The next chapter will contain more clues to the ever-rich soil beneath your feet.

Chapter 5

The World Inside

This chapter will contain the secret sauce to the world's existence and how to obtain complete control over it.

That makes me snicker.

Why?

Because I've known you for long enough to know that this statement doesn't mean what people will think it means.

Exactly how do you think I grab people's attention? I need to keep scaring them into believing there is a secret that is being kept from them. In fact it's true; however, it's not a sinister plan by some maniacal centaur that is hiding the truth from people. The truth is being hidden in plain sight, and like a key in the grass, only those who are looking for it will find it.

So what is "the world inside" as you have named it?

The world inside your mind is what we are getting at. What is your mind?

Oh, come on. I really have to summon an answer to that?

>   Yes. It's a test.

Lovely. Let's see. I know it's not in my brain. We discussed that many times in the past.

>   Yes.

The mind is not my thinking thoughts because that is in my brain.

>   Yes.

My mind is the totality of me—conscious, unconscious, sensory observations, feeling, recall, past lives, present life memories?

>   No. It is none of the above.

Look, it took some measure of thinking to arrive at that answer. I don't think I have another answer in me.

>   Ha. That's what you think. Try again. I'll give you
>   a clue. What makes God into a controllable source of
>   energy?

Faith.

>   What else?

Will?

>   Yes. Very good. What is will?

Will is the courage to do.

>   No.

Can I look it up?

Nope. Work it out. What is the will in the mind of being?

Will is the belief that what is desired is obtainable.

You are correct! If you take this will and put it into the power of God, what is going to happen?

The creative force makes it happen?

What happened?

The desired thing?

No. What happens to the will when it is placed into the power of God?

My wish is your command?

Yes! That is exactly the course of every manner of perfection that comes to shine in the light of being. When will is placed into the power of God, God serves the wish with a mighty force. If the force were any stronger it would blow the poor human apart before the will was done.

Is this superhuman strength they talk about?

Funny. That makes me laugh wholeheartedly. Do you really think it is the human who is doing the extraordinary thing?

Well I used to, but your reaction tells me otherwise.

Super-humans only happen when the force of will is utilized to empower the body. God steps in where physics fails. Where physics fails is where the nature of God overrides the construction of the body, and the mind is using the power of God. The mind is a force field of sorts around the body, and it is connected to the mind of God.

The mind of God is the place where all of the natures of every creature on earth reside—the nature of every animal of the sea, the forest, the desert, the ocean, the air, the plains, and the mountains.

What do you notice about this list?

That there are many environments.

What else?

That each environment has a density of water?

Yes. Even air contains water. What is it about the desert however, that it doesn't have water? We mean, why doesn't it have water?

No trees for the water cycle.

That's right. There are no trees to make the water cycle. Why are there no trees?

I thought that it was because the desert used to be the bottom of the sea. But I don't remember my geology class in college.

The desert is not just a former sea; it is also a former sky.

Dear me. What do you mean?

There was a time in the history of the earth when what was on top is now on bottom and what is now on bottom was once on top. That is indeed where oil comes from, and where all of the rich uranium and topical ointments, all sorts of plastics and petroleum-based products come from. But there is one more thing that comes out of this former sky and former ocean. There is water that comes from this place. The water is clean and fresh and good to drink. But why am I telling you this? Because when the time comes to mine the desert for oil, the water will also come. When that happens, scientists will uncover a rich and abundant ecosystem they have never imagined possible. Inside the desert sand is an oasis of natural resources that can only enhance life on earth, but God will not allow this to happen until the world opens its door to peace, in the Middle East, everywhere peace.

I think I understand where you're going with this. You are showing me the things to come are completely within our control as a race of beings.

Yes. There is a whole new universe opening to the human population, but it will not happen without great change and great responsibility happening on the part of those who are in power.

This takes me to our first lesson for this chapter, which we call reflection.

We've already discussed a form of self-reflection as it pertains to self-awareness. As I mentioned before, God felt the effects firsthand of the question "what am I?"

Boy, is that an understatement.

Well, it's not an understatement; it is a simple statement for a complex set of events that followed suit. What begins to take shape in the very moment of surprise, in the waves of being, is the very construct of becoming. When that construct is tumbling about, new ways of possibility begin to emerge in the flow of everlasting being.

Can you explain what everlasting being is?

Yes. But first you need to notice one other peculiar aspect of the aforementioned.

Do you mean the comment about surprise?

Yes. Surprise is a very important aspect of turning your thoughts inward. Look up the word.

Surprise, "come upon suddenly or unexpectedly."

Yes, but there is a reference you overlook in its origin.

It says in the etymological origin "take napping."

It was originally used as a term to mean take the prize while the owner is napping. This is how I mean the surprise in this event. The napping soldier is the previous state of being. There is no one to guard the fortress in the changing of the guard. When that happens, the one who is napping is away from the soldier's gate, and the one who has come to open the gate is led into the fortress of being. When that occurs, all manners of good fortune arise. The good fortune is the awareness that the one who asks the question "what am I?" is led to the secret garden of internal knowledge.

Why is it a kept secret?

Because when the asker has only the slightest ounce of knowledge of its Self, it has used its environment to define itself. What it saw around it was beauty and grandeur and so it thought its place was to dwell with the spectacle of its own shell. In time however, the spectacle started to show cracks and began to lose its luster in the eyes of the being who had gazed upon it. When the being began to wonder how it had gotten there in the first place, the being began to see there were reasons for things to be and it wanted to know the reason for its own self to be.

When the being asked "what am I?" it gazed within its Self to find the answer, and it noticed something peculiar about its own construction. It found itself deep within the belly of a masterful and brilliant light. This light gave the being more love than it ever imagined possible, and knowing that it was love in this way the being discovered that it was made of love. The love that it was made of was the love that it noticed had constructed all things that the asker had found beautiful and magical. Then the being suddenly realized there was more than one being in this magical light. There were actually many beings in this light. The beings that the asking being noticed were not only beautiful and brilliant but also in the same way of being as it was. And so the little being that asked the question "what am I?" made itself into the light of being, never to wonder again what it was.

That's a beautiful story. What are we to learn from it?

> The waves of being are many. All that you are is made of them. Anything you choose to be is already made within you because it is contained within the secret fortress of who you are.

You know what this reminds me of? It reminds me of the time I read about our DNA. I read that only one percent of our DNA structure is responsible for making us. The rest is just extra.

> No, the rest is not just random extra. The rest is the DNA leftovers of your biological genealogy. It is your family tree, so to speak.

How far back does it go?

> It goes way back to the origins of time. It goes way beyond that as well, but there's no way to prove that in science. The immeasurable realm is just that; immeasurable.
>
> This takes us to our next topic. We're now ready to discuss the nature of mimicry and how that is related to the secret sauce of God's ever present power. Are you ready?

Probably not.

> No problem. Get yourself ready.

~

> Mimicry is the wisest of all beings because it sets aside its own nature long enough to mimic the thing it wants to be. There are creatures on earth that are masters of disguise, but that is not the same as mimicry. When you are looking to become something new, what is the first thing you do?

Research.

> No, you don't. You don't research how to become a wave of being.

My ideas are a little vague here. What do you mean "wave of being."

> The being you are right now is a wave pattern. This wave pattern distinguishes you from other wave patterns. It is why you don't look like a mouse or a fly or a shoe.

A shoe has a wave of being?

Yes, very much so. Every ounce of energy that went into making that shoe produced a wave of being until the hide of the cow was fully made into a new being.

Oh, so a wave of being doesn't have to be living?

A shoe is made from a living being, and that is derived from a desire and the will of the being. This is the construction purpose of shoe being. This is a pretty small example of the nature of being but represents the creative force abundant in order to create a shoe. The shoe is a derivative of the course of creative notions.

Okay, then how do you mean *my* being?

Your being will change with every effort you make toward a new being. All day long you are devising the new being within you and becoming the state of being that is making you. Let me explain.

When God chose to be the light, what did God find in God's self to become light?

Light?

Right. How did I manifest in order to become light?

You overcame the darkness.

Right. So the first step to becoming is to decide to be something.

Yes.

The first step is making a decision, what is the next step?

Overcoming the obstacles?

Not exactly.

Mimic the object you desire?

Not the object you desire, the being you desire.
You mistook the notion of light as an object just as
you mistook the shoe. But what you are skipping in
your analysis is the idea that there is an object to
uncover in the notion of being. This is how humans
think unfortunately, but it's easy to overcome. Let's
discuss the nature of being for a moment.

The nature of being is all about the turning
of time. Time is not the clock. Time is the cycles of
manifestation. Every cell has a manifesting schedule.
This schedule is in the rapid movement of organelles
to work toward the end cycle. The end cycle is the
completion of the new being. Every cell has the very
necessity to enrich its own resources in order to fulfill the task at hand. This task is that of satisfying the
will of the mind. So how this relates to mimicry is by
reflecting on the desired being that comes from decision and mimicking the way it looks. You are your own
holographic machine. You are producing the external
mechanisms that produce a new being.

I need an example, please.

Let's say you decide you want to be an astronaut.
When you make that decision, you have already stud-
ied astronauts because otherwise you would not have
decided to become one. So what you then do is mimic
one. You study what they study, you train how they
train, you work where they work, and so on. This is a
simple example of a long process of becoming.

How is this the secret sauce?

The secret sauce is in the nature of mimicry as it pertains to the miraculous events that occur in the cells: the mirroring effect of self to not self upon those who represent the new self. The new self represents the state of becoming, in the process of creating. If you let that sink into your mind a little bit, I'm sure you'll see the event horizon.

I can't see it, I'm terribly sorry. Three days from now when I read this, it will be clear as day, but not right now.

The new self is related to the mirroring effect. You transition from one state to the next merely by imagining yourself there. The cells only work on your behalf and take the imagined being into the real state of being. This process of becoming utilizes the nature of mimicry because each cell claims its position in the process to meet the demands of the will of being.

Thank you. That is much clearer.

I'm only here to serve your understanding; I'm not here to alarm or confuse you. Now I have one last measure of meaning to give you before we close this chapter.

~

Okay I think I can absorb some more power talk. I just took a nap, had a snack, and drank some delicious iced tea. I'm refreshed and ready.

Great. I suspect you are prepared only for the deepest part of this chapter?

Lay it on me.

We are now going to discuss how revelation of the soul relates to mimicry and reflection.

Revelation of the soul, that sounds interesting.

Yes, let's quickly recap what happens to being when it works the process of creation. The process of creation begins with the question "what am I?" In the asking there is a wave of being that turns on the soul. The soul is literally awakening from its slumber and begins to seek the asker.

The asker soon finds it is not alone in its body. The way of noticing this is by remembering the core of human worth. The core of human worth stands at the door of enlightenment when the asker looks inward for information about the ever-present source of its nature. This natural source is a spring of worth, a spring of fresh and purified being.

God, this just sounds like science fiction or fantasy fiction.

Science fiction and fantasy fiction are actually inspired by real events. You must understand that the imagination is an incredible power connected to the real realms of God and mortal being. Some of what you notice in science fiction precedes actual science. You don't think it works the other way around?

You mean where actual events precede the fiction? I never thought of it that way, no.

Well trust me. You already know more about the realms of being than you think, only because some writer has given you stories. The stories are many times real manifestations in the realm of universal being.

Let's get back to revelation of the soul.

The soul is revealed to the asker, and at the connecting mirror there is a truth that is told to reveal the weight of the talents in the gifts of the asker's ways.

So are you saying that we face ourselves when we ask what we are?

Precisely. This is not always a happy occasion. This often is one of the hardest events in a person's life. To face the soul is to reveal every ounce of energy you have put forth into the making of the soul's ways of being. If you have been good to yourself, your soul will not be sullied. But if you have struggled and badgered, roughed-up and beaten your soul in order to survive, you will see the destruction in how your soul looks back at you.

This is where some people run from themselves, continually finding a way to not have to face their own tragedies. The more they run, however, the further behind their soul becomes in the evolution to spirit. The soul can be restored, quite literally. Having the courage to walk up to your soul and say, "I'll make this right, I'll treat you the way you deserve, I'll protect you and strengthen you and give you the time you need."

That's when the whole world changes. That's when the soul awakens to a new day and opens the way of the heart. That's when it knows it is protected, and in the spring that comes the soul is awakened in joy.

There is one last thing I want for you to understand about the soul awakening. What is the truth about God and the soul?

Can I have a clue?

Sure. What truth is God?

God is light.

Yes. Make that now what truth is the soul.

Soul is light.

Yes. But it can be taken over by darkness. It can be overshadowed by darkness.

Can it overcome the dark the way God did?

Absolutely. But the struggle is inevitable and the struggle for light is a worthy one. No need to take this thought further for now. We will find a way to awaken the soul to light in upcoming chapters that teach the way of the universe.

Chapter 6

The World According to God

When the world began its manner of searching for the ways of its own making, it began a destiny that was foretold. It began a search into the ways of creation by the very struggle of making a worthier life than the one of the worth of God. When that search began, there was no God to give the world direction. The world's direction became one of never-ending duty. This duty was in the toil and the toil had no meaning.[1]

One day God decided it was time to introduce the purpose that the world had forgot. In this day there was a mighty wind. This wind was strong and full of destruction.[2]

When calm became the world again, all that was left was a few manners of worldly makings. These few manners were those of rock and stone. What stood before the gentle creatures that survived was a temple of doom, and in it were two works from the previous dwellers. These works represented the light of God and the darkness of the doom and despair of never-ending sorrow.[3]

When the manners of destruction had made the course of the world into a worshipping work, there was nothing but the remnants of light to lead the new world out of its doom.[4]

Is this an historical occurrence?

> Not in the way you mean. This story is one that has yet to occur. It has a story about what happens to a world that forgets its manner of purpose. When there is no purpose in the ways of a man or a woman, the way of wind will wipe clean the work that was done for no reason other than to toil.
>
> When the work of God is unknown to the creatures that God makes, then there is a destructive pattern that winds up consuming itself.
>
> This is not a punishment; it is just a natural course of nature. Everything that dwells in the patterns of God must serve a purpose or it becomes unnecessary to the existence within which it became.
>
> What is your question? We sense some worthy questions coming forth.

When you are saying that each creature must serve a purpose, I imagined the balance of nature in how everything seems to be dependent upon something else in nature, in order to survive.

> This balance is exactly why there is a purpose that must be served in the course of a life. For each life that makes its home in the waves of being there is a true case of the ways of God working on behalf of the ways of another being.
>
> One being may be overwrought with predation. When the urge to survive becomes so strong that the being that is overwrought with danger imagines a way to survive, God takes a hammer to the ways of the predator and teaches it how to stop overeating. One way may be to increase the population of its enemy. Another may be to decrease its food supply. One other way may be to create a new predator to destroy the creature's overbearing way.

This reminds me of the effects of an alien plant or fish species that is introduced into non-native environments. It becomes aggressive and takes over where the environment has not developed resistance to its aggression.

> Exactly. The correction to this does not happen overnight. These changes take a long time to occur. If you imagine it, you'll see that the ways of animals in evolution have changed to become more gentle, less beastly over time.

It does appear that prehistoric animals are no longer around. And the dinosaurs, with their terrifying teeth and size, have disappeared from the earth.

> These are indeed aspects of evolution that show a softening of the nature of beasts. Humans as well with all of their power of destruction have been declawed or defanged; an increase in their size has been because God saw fit to make them giants on the earth. But the ultimate giants of the animal world are certainly not the humans.

May I ask you where you are going with this? I guess the urge for purpose is showing through in my impatience to get to the point.

> Right. But there is also another urge in your way: the urge to know. What did we start this chapter with?

A story about the world searching for the ways of its own making, which I'm not really sure I understand.

> Your question then is "what is the world of its own making?"

Yes.

Let's start there and work back to the point of this chapter. "The world of its own making" has a connotation to it. What is it?

World means "the age of man." So, the age of man is searching to become self-aware?

Yes. It is looking for what it *is* and what it must become. But there was something that happened in this world that caused destruction, what was it?

There was no God?

Yes. There was no will above what the world willed upon itself. Why is this destructive?

It sounds self-defeating, but I'm not sure why I get that feeling.

The reason there is a self-defeating ring to it is because the wave of being is circled back onto its own course.

It sounds like a centrifuge.

Yes. A tornado is another way of thinking of it.

Is a tornado a symbol of self-destruction?

Not hardly. It is a literal form of self-annihilation.

You seem to be warning the world that if it doesn't change course, nature will change to destroy human population.

No, I'm not saying that. I'm saying that humans cause their own destruction when there is no worth in their toil, beyond the ways of their own being. There is a literal effect in the way nature consumes that which serves no purpose of its own.

I'm not sure I can formulate the question in my mind. I don't see the connection between the mindless toil of human beings and the ultimate response from nature.

> You have not asked the question you want to ask.

What is the connection between human behavior and the annihilation of the human race?

> That is not the question. The question you are trying to ask is what causes tornadoes? The weather or humankind?

Yes! That is the question.

> Well it is not nature alone, and it is not humans alone. But it is the natural phenomenon that occurs when the conditions are right. So here's the way it happens.
> Tornadoes make the cycles of weather patterns as much as weather patterns make tornadoes. If there were some way to see where a tornado is going to land, then there would be some way to avoid death, right?

Yes.

> But what if there was no way to know how to escape one?

I guess you would have to succumb to the inevitable.

> Well, okay, but that doesn't answer my question. What if there was no way to know how to escape a tornado?

You would learn how to survive it?

> No.

Your question is not the same as asking what if there is no way to escape one. You are asking what if there is no way to *know* how to escape one.

> Yes. This is a different question. I am asking about knowledge.

The instinct to survive would keep you searching for a way, if tornados constantly plagued you.

> Yes. This is the course of evolution and how the nature of will is so powerful. That is the answer to the riddle, but now let's get back to how that relates to purpose.
>
> Purpose is the very construct of creation, or you may prefer evolution if you don't believe in purpose. But creation relies solely on the need to create a survival game. The problem with what has happened to the world is that it has lost its sense of purpose. And when a sense of purpose is forgotten, then the powers of destruction are *not* kept at bay, because there is no need to find a way to survive. Survival then will depend on the destructive power of nature to remind the human world of its frailty in the wake of all that ever was.

All that ever was—that has a ring of the infinite.

> Infinite is a course for the evolving state of being.

It's not clear to me what that means.

> Infinite is a process, a verb, not a thing.

Cool.

> There is one more wave of knowing for this chapter, and it's not going to be very easy for you, or your

readers, because it will go against everything you believe to be true. And it has to do with the focus of God on mortal man.

God is not convinced that mortal man is in the wake of its own nature anymore. What we mean is that man has become so consumed by his own world that he may not be able to survive his own creation.

Please elaborate.

There has been a polluting of the seas, a destruction of the trees, a working environmental disaster that cannot be overlooked any longer. This overlooked destruction has come in the form of how the world grows its food and how it keeps the animals that God puts forth on the earth for man's benefit. Man has completely forgotten to grace the planet with nutrients to replace what is being removed in the soil. The kinds of nutrients that are being used are synthetic replacements, and that will cause a cycle of fake food. Man must stop making fake food and fake nutrients for the soil. There is no way to promise any future for humankind if man continues to rob the body of its necessary nutrients. To make synthetic soil is to make synthetic bodies.

This will require so many thousands of years of evolution to overcome, that populations will one day become resistant to any form of anti-disease-making cells. This is because the synthetic parts of the body will not respond to the current ways of nature to heal the body. The cells in the body are so dependent on certain nutrients that when they don't get them, there will be an abundance of cancers too numerous to treat, if the humans don't get really serious about the way they feed the planet. Not only in how the planet feeds its population, but also in how it feeds itself in the soil.

There is such a destruction of balance going on that God wonders how long humans have before they greatly reduce the populations to nothing more than obese, cancer-ridden mules with only one purpose.

What purpose is that?

To eat.

This is a very grim look at our world.

It is, in God's view, "counterbalanced."

How so?

Counter-balanced is not what you think it is. You think there is another weightier way that is causing the shift toward annihilation. You think there is more causing man's destruction than just his misguided attempts to play God.

I do?

Yes you do. Think for a moment. Do you not hope I am wrong?

Yes. I do.

Do you not think that science will come up with an argument that you cannot counter?

If you mean counter with the wisdom you are giving me, then yes.

Well then, there is a counterbalance happening. God's view of the world is counterbalanced by man's unending drive toward a market economy-driven world. Man will have every reasonable explanation under the sun, and because humans are so sense-centered, these reasonable people with money-managed lives will make perfect sense to you. And you will forget the contents of this book on a day when the world goes belly-up in the stock market. Again the world will fret and worry, fret and worry about something that occurs over a single cycle, and again the world will forget its purpose and forget the eons of time that made the world in the first place. This is what is so crazy about man's world. Until the cycle of doom has run its course, man is destined for destruction, and God will not stop it, for what is God to do? What is God to make of mankind that he refuses to make of himself?

It is time now to end this chapter and allow these notions to settle in. You will find the next chapter to uncover the soul of man and to give it a new course that could avoid the deadly system it has fallen into.

Chapter 7

The Soul Emerges When the Mind of God Is Not Forgotten

The only way to remove the damage of doom and despair is to know the soul and its personal journey toward Spirit.

When God opens the door to man what does man find?

I'm only guessing at this, based on the image that emerged in my head.

Go ahead. You know we will correct you if you are wrong.

This is true. I imagined the amazing images that have come from the Hubble telescope.

But guess what? You are wrong.

Of course.

Try again.

When God opens the door to man, man finds himself?

No.

What door is God opening again?

Good question! It could have been your first question, but you chose not to ask because you assumed you were supposed to know the answer already.

You know me too well.

Right, I do. What you want to know is what door does God open to man, and the answer is the door to the universe.

So the question is, when God opens the door to the universe to man, what does man find?

That's the question.

Well, man finds something bigger than himself, for one thing.

Oh my, not only bigger than himself but bigger than anything he can imagine ever fully knowing in his lifetime.

Right.

What else does he discover?

How about a clue?

Okay. What is your wave of being relative to the wave of the universe?

A tiny, tiny blip on the cycles of time . . .

How much do you think of that universe is your own imagination?

Well, I guess all of it. I'm imagining relative time because billions of light years are inconceivable.

No, you're not imagining relative time, you are imagining relative space. These are different things.

Relative time is the mastered way of knowing that A and B are related to one another. A is you and B is the universe.

A and B are a distance between each other that makes you uneventful, relative to the events of space. Space, therefore, is imagined because you cannot actually measure it. The same way as if you were to know exactly what time you emerged in space relative to the time that all of the aspects of space have emerged.

Okay. I'm not seeing the point here.

The point is that time is not the location of your being. It is, however, the coordinates of your soul relative to your imagination.

Still don't follow.

Have you made your life-way a set of principles relative to space?

I think you mean the space between things. The answer is no, I don't believe so.

Then how do you know you exist?

I have tangible evidence.

Right, but let's suppose you were not a body that could give you tangibility.

You mean if I was only a mind, for example?

Right. As if you had no sense organs to give you tangible relativity.

Meaning, I didn't know the space I occupied.

Exactly.

Then I guess my existence would be immeasurable.

It would not only be immeasurable, it would be un-provable.

I see. So where are we going with this?

The wave of your being would not only have an un-provable level of existence, it would also have the ways of force because nothing would affect your being. There would be nothing to act upon, nor anything to act upon you.

Therefore, the nature of your being could move across the open waves of manner[1], without having anything to stop you.

Okay.

Then if nothing could stop you, you could also have extraordinary relevance to the space you didn't occupy.

You see where we're going yet?

Not yet, exactly.

Where do you think this conversation is leading?

You seem to be describing God.

Yes, we are. We are describing the incredible lightness of Being . . . your being, all being, God being.

So the mind of God is an unstoppable Being?

Yes. This is the point we are making. And so when the mind of God is relevant to the nature of the forces of ways of being, there is an emergence of soul.

You lost me. How does the soul emerge from the mind of God?

> When we look at the last chapter, where humanity is in the course of its own destruction, what emerges?

Soul?

> Yes, and how is that possible?

When there is no body to define the space?

> Right. When space has no relevance, the one that "needs to survive" is gone. Survival is no longer an urge. What then is left over to make the soul prove that it exists?

I don't know.

> Exactly. You don't know. How could you know if you're still a body? There is no proof of the soul to the body, because the body must prove its existence by the tangible evidence that it does, indeed, exist. It is constantly reassuring itself through the process of relationship: relevance between that which it is, and that which it is not. Why, then, do you think there is a purpose for the body?

To give the soul proof of existence?

> Bingo!

Wow. But the soul has a problem.

> What is that?

The body doesn't believe the soul exists.

> This is the conundrum, and yet it is the purpose of the body to discover the soul.

And how does it do that?

> The way the body discovers the soul is by verifying that there is something more to life than merely existing. The body's complete and utter existence depends on its connection to the mind of God. When the mind of God is finally found, it is the soul that is remembering the value of its true essence.

So in order to find the soul, one must find God?

> No. One must find the *mind* of God. The mind of God is in the ways of the soul.

So you don't have to find God to find your soul?

> No. Not really. Finding God is actually impossible because God is everything that ever was, so how do you find that?

Well, I see your point, but how is that different than finding the mind of God?

> The mind of God exists in you.

So we find our own mind of God?

> Yes. Each and every living thing contains a piece of the mind of God.

So we just have to find our own piece and we can discover our soul?

> Yep. It's that simple.

Is that the end of this chapter?

> No. Just the beginning . . . now that you understand why the body exists, it's time to understand

why the soul exists and why it's important to make
the ways of God relevant to the ways of man on earth.

~~~

I put the pen down and went to bed. The morning came soon
and I pulled my body out of the cool, cotton sheets and quilt-
ed summer blanket. I am staying at my friend's casita on the
Guadalupe River. She's given me the place to write on week-
ends. It's a record hot August. Balmier still under the shade
of water oaks and bald cypress trees; their exposed roots like
boney fingers reach into the soil and rock below. These roots
hold tight as the river's current moves constantly past. The
song of the cicada bares witness to the dry, West Texas land
that surrounds this oasis. I have the benefit of a wooden deck
from which to view the cool river below. I eat my breakfast
of two fried eggs, canned black beans, and yellow-corn torti-
llas. As I sip morning coffee I'm watching a couple drift down
stream in a canoe. The quiet is then broken again as a fly fish-
erman and his three young sons appear. They each cast their
lines with less grace than he, the smallest boy tries to catch up,
pleading for them to wait as he plants one unsure foot after
the other navigating the rocks in the riverbed.

Here I am separated from my husband and his son whom
I have made my own. They go on with domestic life in my
absence. On this deck I don't think about my job on Monday.
Monday I will write about the intricate workings of engineer-
ing marvels, such that carve and drill into the earth to extract
oil six miles below the ocean floor. But the marvels I write
about this weekend have taken eons to develop and are of immeasurable worth. And when I go back to work in two days,
I will not forget this time that dwells deep in the mind of
creation. The time it has taken to gestate these moments has
been a short lifetime, yet in this moment, I am stalling. I am
stalling because I know the words that come next will again

shatter the walls of dimension. Again I will stand face-to-face with what I didn't know, with what the world doesn't know. This troubles me because the burden to share it feels like a mighty finger on my back, moving me gently forward while my feet drag behind.

> Very nicely said.

Thank you?

> Yes, what's wrong with the compliment?

Nothing at all. Thank you.

> Let's get to the task at hand shall we?

Of course.

> You now know that life is in the balance when man has made his life counter to God's path of nature.

Yes. That, too, is difficult news to hear; quite a damning assessment to have made of our world.

> There is no running from it, I'm afraid. There is no way to change the course of man, if he continues to work his way against the natural balance of God. There *is* a way however, for humans to save their soul and when the soul has been saved from the powers of darkness, which rule against the light, then there is hope to change the way that humans interact with the earth.

Working from the inside out rather than outside in?

> Precisely. This is why God makes the chore of learning so difficult for man. The way man works is to take what he sees and internalize it. The way that

God works in man is to take what is internal and bring it to the world.

God, can I ask an unrelated question?

Shoot.

When I was in college, I hated seeing the word "man" used as a general statement about humans because as a woman I could not see myself in that word. The word *man,* to me, evoked images of males only and it was a difficult battle to fight in my sense of who I was. It doesn't bother me so much anymore, but I worry for youngwomen readers.

Ah yes, the man/woman thing. Let's take a side note here to discuss this unusual event in the course of humankind.

Event?

Yes. This will get you intrigued. You were not always a race of male/female. Humans were once androgynous creatures that lived between the construct of spirit and the construct of physical being. You were not even a race of beings that were able to make your own kind without having the inevitable worth of God interfere.[2] This was because only God could make you. That's why when God decided it was time for man to have a partner, we made woman.

Woman was made from the rib of man for a very important reason. Her job was to protect the heart of God and the breath of life in man. That is why we made her from the ribcage.

So man did not have a penis originally?

Nope. Not even the notion of fertility. Man was just a simple being made from earth and spirit.

Did we evolve from primates?

> Not in the way science describes it. There is no family tree that links man directly from primates, because there were so many half-human half-other species before the primate version.

What?! Like on the Egyptian hieroglyphs?

> No, those are not, fortunately, the experiments we are referring to, but they do represent the story we are telling you now.

Why fortunately?

> It is your good fortune that you were not a race of creatures that began with Egyptians. Egyptians were tyrants toward the mortal creatures who inhabited the land. They were of a magical race, but brutal in conquest. That's another book.
>
> Yes, there were other natural experiments of half-man creatures, but they did not appear on earth, they appeared in middle-earth a long, long, long, time ago.

This sounds like a different book also. Should I refrain from questions?

> No, we can tie this truth into the nature of man's soul very easily. You see what this is telling you is that what you see on earth is only the small end of the pyramid.

The capstone?

> Indeed. Middle-earth is the rest of it.

You mean as far as this planet is concerned?

Right. We aren't going to talk about the other planets for now. What we are leading you toward is the version of the story that will save man's soul in the course of his physical annihilation.

God, can I ask how long this destruction is going to take?

Not long.

From now?

Not long even in the eyes of man.

I feel like Noah when you told him of a great flood.

You got it.

Got what?

You have the idea. There is no way to avoid destruction, and it won't take more than a few generations until mankind has reached its limit to what it can take.

In what sense?

The body cannot withstand all of the natural attacks that will come after it, if it remains in a state of fear and want. The disease that the body becomes plagued by is absolutely in the conquest of its ever-evolving spirit, so it eats the body away to find the source of creation.

You mean the way we dig into the earth to find the origins of time, disease digs at the layers of the body?

Not just the human body, all bodies. It is a cellular urge to know. The way that God once did when the big bang occurred, that is the urge of all that exists.

As destructive as that is, it's really kind of cool.

> You know, I thought you would like that.

So let's go back to the soul and how man can save himself.

> He can't save *himself*. He must save the *soul* that inhabits his body.

I may need a little clarification.

> Man is not just soul; he is also a world unto himself. This world was given to him when there was no one around who could account for the natural beings that began filling up the earth's crust. There was a time when nature had become so overrun with so many creatures that God needed a way to account for them. Mortal man was created to do this job. He/she/it, whatever you want to call the first human being to walk the earth, was in a state of complete union with God. Man's purpose was to begin describing, defining, explaining what was on the earth.

Why wouldn't God already know?

> Well, it's hard to explain . . . because the mind is so expansive it is only when the consciousness is triggered by the observable is the manner of mind able to remember. When the mind forgets any aspect of the original notions, it is as if the notion does not exist. And so God needed the reminding mind, which in this case was man. He was created completely purposefully. He was by no means an afterthought on the chain of evolution. He was created to keep the essence of God conscious on the surface of the earth.

Genesis talks about that, "whatsoever Adam called every living creature, that was the name thereof."

Yes, this is the story that man was told in another time in history when the world was consumed by its own fashion of ill-reward. It was a time in history very similar to today.

Man was saved?

In a sense he was. But what was different then was that he had not devised a way to destroy himself that was so difficult to come back from. Remember, this time the problems are deep within the ways that man grows food. This is intrinsically counter-productive to the living capability of God on earth. You cannot interfere with Mother Nature and expect to rise victorious. Nature is eons older and worthy of knowing the patterns of her own process much better than man, trust me.

I do.

Good. Now back to the soul that inhabits man's body. There is a way to understand it, but forgive me for having to be symbolic. Because there is no literal explanation possible, until your brain has words for the literal occurrence. When you have developed words that work, I'll be able to tell you this in a way that science can confirm for you, but for now the story must serve to inform over literal ways of speaking.

I'm good with that.

The story we will tell is about the nature of God working inside the mortal nature, while the body develops in the womb.

Cool!

When woman consults her soul and finds herself in the way of baby and working mechanisms, she works to accumulate all of her resources to give the new body life. These resources include her blood for nutrients, her waves of grain for what we call firmament, and she also gives her precious mortal essence. This essence is a magical manner of lifting the work above the waves of being and into the way of God. The waves of being have to be forgotten, if you remember, in order to become.

She raises her essence to the way of God by knowing there is a purpose in finding she is to be a woman with child. If this purpose of being is given to the child, then the child's soul will inhabit the body with full intention. If the baby is not given a purpose, if it is unwanted by the mother, or if there is no benefit to the earth for its coming, the soul that inhabits the body will not have any purpose for coming. A soul without purpose is a misguided soul. A misguided soul can easily grow to encumber its own progress in its evolution of spirit when the world that it is entering has no purpose of its own, other than to toil without end.

I'm feeling a little dense again; can you define a few things for me?

Sure. You are with one woman who can answer all of your questions, though.

Me?

Yes. She is more capable than she lets on. Let her have a go.

Alright. So I think you are saying that when a mother is able to know a child's purpose, then that is passed on to the baby's development in the womb?

Yes.

And so this child is raised in an environment that can overcome the lack of purpose in the world.

Yes.

If however, the mother sees no purpose in the child being born, it will not be able to overcome the lack of purpose the world provides.

No, this is not exactly true. There are mechanisms of God throughout. If the child is able to recognize that the world serves no purpose for his soul and he is filled with questions, eventually his questions can lead him to the rightful way of knowing himself.

But the mother can provide a head start?

Yes. But more importantly, she provides a sense of belonging. Belonging is the essence of God. Belonging is the feeling that all is perfection. It is a peaceful feeling that rises in one, which leads one to joy.

I see. So where do we go from here?

This is why the soul exists, to inform the body of where it is to go, where it is to be, and how it is to fulfill its sense of purpose. When that is discovered, the soul moves in unison with the body to make the origins of man a purpose of its own.

You mean finding our origin is the purpose of existence?

Yes. Let's say man's world suddenly understood its purpose. What would he be doing? He would be striving toward knowing. He would be evacuating every construct that avoids the light; and he would be pursuing the ways of knowing. He would be asking the continual question that God once asked God's self.

What am I?

Yes. That is all he need do. And in the course of his asking, he would uncover his extraordinary worth in the realm of God and perpetuate the resources of that which made him whole. When God fulfills this within man, man knows where he belongs, and when he knows where he belongs, his spirit evolves.

This reminds me of the philosophers of old and the original meaning of the word *university*. It came from seeking knowledge and man finding his place in the universe.

Yes, there were times in human history when man was on target to uncover the secrets of the soul, and it will come again because it is a natural course.

Sounds like the origin of "course work."

Yes. Course work means in the course of knowing.

Is this the end of this chapter?

One last thing. There is no way to know the soul when the body is around. It can only become a summoned entity, but it is unknowable because the body seeks its own awareness. It is a conundrum.

So is that why faith is important?

Chapter 8

When the Universe Was Made, the World of Man Was Designed

The title of this chapter already has me confused, because man on earth came a long time after the big bang.

> Well then here goes another eye opener. The world of man does not relate to the origins of the universe until the man of worth becomes aware of his origins.

So there is a play on words in this title?

> Exactly. Let's begin. What is the nature of making?

To bring into being.

> Yes. How does "bring into being" affect the nature of God?

God is becoming?

> Yes. The nature of becoming is the way of being, in its state of moving ever so. Moving ever so is the way that God is in all things. So how does God's nature move through human beings?

By evolving man's being?

> Not quite, but close. Try again.

By evolving the man's spirit?

> Getting closer.

By evolving the mortal soul to spirit?

> What is the signature in this way?

How do you mean signature? I think I know, but I can't articulate it.

> The signature in the way that something moves is the vibrational course. Its signature is the remnant of its course.

So, you are asking me 'what is the remnant signature of moving soul to spirit?'

> Yes.

Is it something about material and light?

> No.

It's times like these I wish I was a physicist. I'm sure there is some equation that would help me.

> Yes there is, but it is not the only way to understand this event in the course of evolution. Give yourself the credit to know that the answer is on the tip of your tongue.

In moving soul to spirit there is a rising of the vibrational signature?

Yes. It is exactly that and nothing more. When the soul is manifested from the disappearance of the body, the next stage of its evolution is to adhere to the movement signature of God. This is what is called spirit.

Spirit moves throughout all of the being of all of the constructs of the universe. It is in this movement that all lower forms of vibration fall out of. The lower forms of vibration fall out of spirit in order to become individual. This is how singularity becomes duplicity with each course of ways of individuals. The importance here is to understand what the original design of man is.

The original design is the casting set of principles. It is casting in the sense of making a mold. God did not just allow man to form; God designed man's form. But in this sense we are not talking about man's body; we are talking about man's soul. Soul, once again, is formless. The only way to replicate God's nature is to create a formless notion of light. Light is just a way however, of describing the essence of the soul that is related to God. God does not make anything out of nothing. The material of the soul is God material. That material is co-mingled with earth matter to create the substance from which man's world is derived.

Man's world is an attempt to recreate God for a reason. Everything man does on earth is a replicating urge to imagine God. So when man works the soil, or builds the fortresses for his domain, or makes movement through vehicles, he's driven to do so through the mechanisms of God's creative power.

Now let's step back a moment and look at what makes it possible for human form to exist, since we have already stated that God makes what God is as God becomes.

I'm ready.

> What you find in your way is God moving the forces of being around until the waves of being are created.

This sentence is a bit confusing, "what you find in your way," you mean my way personally or is that a general "you?"

> This will just have to be a complex component of these dialogues. Language is very, very limiting, so follow along until I can break up the understandable elements and then reassemble them for you.

Okay, thanks for seeing my problem.

> Not a problem at all, just a complex aspect of communicating through words. There are so many better ways, but this is the only one that reaches many people at once. But it is also the easiest to get confused.
>
> The course of God is "the way." The way of God is the manner, and the manner of God is what is revealed in the cause and effect principle. So when the universe was revealed to God's awareness of God's self, the building blocks of creation were revealed. The creative means of God's nature was provided and the "hands of God," so to speak, began a process of mastery.
>
> What then is the way that the universe works that causes the bodies of planets and stars to revolve in an orbital pattern?

Are you kidding? I have to devise an answer to that?

> You already know the answer; you learned it in your science classes.

Years ago!

> Just try.

If memory serves, it is the gravitational pull of mass spinning in space.

> Good. Now how is gravity affecting the mass in the center of each object in space?

I am guessing that there is far less gravitational pull on the center than on the surface.

> Not exactly what I'm asking, but I know what you are trying to say. You are trying to say that the axis of the center is stationary to the outer portion of the sphere.

Yes, I think that's what I'm feeling when I try to imagine it.

> It is, trust me.
>
> There is a purpose for that stationary axis. Its purpose is to give direction to the orbital pattern of the manners of spheres. Meaning any change in the axis will mean a change in the orbital pattern.

Okay.

> The orbital pattern is completely managed by this axis. And the axis is completely managed by the movement of God.
>
> Now reread this difficult line and tell me what I meant: "What you find in your way is God moving the forces of being around until the waves of being are created."

Wow! Are you saying you move the planets around until they are orbiting at just the right position for making things come into being?

Yes. You nailed it.

That is so amazing!

The reason this is done is because the discovery
of being came into existence when the world of man
came along.

You lost me again. That sounds like you're saying nature was
accidental until man showed you what was possible.

No, that is not what I said at all.

Okay then, will you say what you said in a way I can understand?

Sure. Man made God.

Now I know that sentence is going to get taken out of context,
and atheists will rejoice while fundamentalists will crucify me!

Ha. Funny. But yes you are correct that that statement does not mean what it appears to mean.
Man is a mind that has the power to become self-
aware. No, man is not the only species that is self-
aware, but for the sake of discussion it is the only one
I'm mentioning.
When a mind is self-aware, it becomes self-made.
It recognizes its freedom from the source of governance and moves to create all that it can in order to
know itself. What, then, happened to man is that man
made God.

Ahh! I see now. God comes into being through man when
man frees himself from anything that governs him.

Not exactly, because that's like saying free from
governance is free from responsibility, and we've
already discussed how responsibility is the sole pur-

pose of living. You must accept responsibility or you do not exist. Remember, if you cannot respond, you must deny, and denial is running from the laws of existence. Let's get back to how man makes God.

Can you make a more truthful statement to your previous one?

I'll try. When man becomes self-aware, he disconnects himself from the source of governance that controls his behavior.

You're getting there, keep going.

He (or she of course) . . .

Of course.

. . . then moves from the forces that control him to controlling the forces of creation.

Exactly. This is God: "the movement of the controls of creation."

So in this sense we replicate the manner of God.

Indeed. But there are some rules of conduct that must be adhered to, because the laws of nature cannot be messed with without some level of jeopardy plaguing the manners of creative means. In other words, even God cannot avoid these laws without a shift in the balance of nature to govern the laws of physics.

You mean you can govern the laws of physics?

Exactly. The way that is done is by recognizing the simple mechanisms that are inherent in the rules of space.

Do you mean space between things?

Yes. It is the space between "things," as you call it, which governs the rules of physics. When I manipulate this space, the cause and effect is directly proportionate to the level of activity between the objects that I move. So the grand design is a simple matter of moving objects in space and the proportionate laws come into play.

It sounds like there are fixed laws of ratio.

No, not fixed but manipulate-able only when the outcome is known. If there is no known outcome, the manner of chaos will interfere with a whole host of variables. So the sole reason for this discussion is that there are no accidents, there is no playing the dice, because I have already seen the destruction that that causes is my universe. It is evident in the explosions of stars in the cosmos and of course what you refer to as black holes. These dark places in the universe are caused by a lack of design on my part. They are what happened when I did not consider the outcome of my own behavior in the creative means. But they were not mistakes, just miscalculations.

Does God ever say, "oops"?

No. That's funny. That is not possible anyway.

Why?

Because as I said, there are no accidents, there is just lack of intention. The design of cause and effect is a perfect principle, not a mistake.

So how does all of this relate to the soul and the spirit?

Okay, here we go. The "master plan" is what you might call it. If the soul is the portion of God that inhabits the body, and the purpose of the body is to recognize the soul, then what is the mechanism in the universal laws of creation that makes the soul the equivalent to God?

I'm going to work this out one word at a time.

Go for it.

First, can I compare the human body to bodies in space?

No.

Can I compare the cells in the body to bodies in space?

Yes.

When the cells in the body recognize they are a Self, a body, the question the body asks itself is 'what moves the body?'

Keep going . . .

When the body recognizes that something other than the world outside of itself is moving it, the body looks within and sees the soul.

Yes, keep going . . .

When the soul is recognized by the body, the soul is given existence.

Yes. Yes. Yes. Have you figured out what comes next?

When the soul is given existence, it discovers its purpose for being.

Yes, one more thing yet.

When it discovers its purpose for being, it finds belonging in the realm of God.

> Yes. That is the total and complete recipe for saving the mortal soul from doom and despair. Because suddenly, the being you are no longer needs the world to survive, and the world can die away and you will live eternal life!

With God?

> Yes, my love, with me in joy and peace and complete in all manner of Being.

So is that the end of the chapter?

> Not yet. One last thing, just to summarize the waves of being in order to manipulate the soul that you have now discovered exists.
>
> The way the soul uncovers its purpose is by moving now with the body in unison. The body has a new life because it discovers it is precious and very, very special to its original being. The original being is the soul, and the soul moves with purpose to protect the body from disease and from danger. The soul lives in a realm that can sense every manner of being outside of the body and inside the body. When the body learns of this new protection, it will in turn become protective of the soul. No longer can toxic people enter its realm without immediate danger alarms going off. Very quickly the body learns to avoid the toxicity of servants of the dark force (this is not the devil, just the absence of the light being). The body will also begin to avoid other toxins, or if the toxic manners continue, they are not tolerated as easily. There is another more incredible thing that happens.

The body learns the rewards of kindness. Kindness to others and kindness to the Self become a two-way street.

This is where we will end this chapter. Next we will talk about the mechanisms of kindness and how important they are to the fulfillment of the soul.

Chapter 9

The Fulfillment of the Soul and the Kindness of Being

When God made mortal man in the image of God, it was not that God made man to look like God but to *be* like God. This is a good place to describe the nature of "we" and the nature of "I." "I am" and "we are" are the constructs of Being in the sense that mortal man is "I will" and "I do."

Man did not attend to God in the beginning of his human existence. There was a time when mortal man (the time before woman was made) that man had to find his own way to God. This happened because God cannot *will* upon any creature the existence of God's manner. This manner must be acknowledged through surrender. The reason for this is because man would not be able to know himself as a human being if he were simply an automaton for God. It is only when mortal man uses his mechanism for good that the kindness of God can occur.

Look up the word "kind."

Do you want the etymological reference?

Yes.

It derives from the meaning child or son.

What else does it say in the original meaning?

In the "archaic" use: a.) origin, b.) nature, c.) manner; way—is how 'kind' is listed.

> This is a good place to start; we will work toward the modern references later.
>
> If you remember your learning from the story of Genesis, there is a reference to animals "each one after their kind."

I remember.

> Well, that's not the way it happened, but I want you to imagine how it's referenced. Each one after its own kind is a meaning that refers to kinship. The connected manner of kinship is the version of the word kindness that I want you to hold in your mind.

Okay.

> Kindness therefore refers to family. The family of man is the family of God because man was created in God's own image.

I understand, but this sounds really biblical.

> Well, is there a pattern you see here?

You mean in spite of the biblical reference?

> No, *because* of it.

Are you saying the story of Genesis is an accurate portrayal of the origin of man?

> No, of course I'm not. The story of Genesis, or what's left of it, is not what I'm getting at. I'm asking you to look deep into the mind of God for a moment

and see a pattern of kindness/kinship, animals, and God as they relate to the origin of man.

I'm not sure I'm following, but if God is without form and man is created in God's likeness, is he not also without form in this reference?

> You are indeed following, because before man was made in form, man was made in soul. The soulful nature of God is the soulful nature of mankind.

So this precedes the time on earth?

> Yes. It is the time before time. When God says time, remember it is not the way of the clock but of the cycles of the universe. So the original story of Genesis, before it was stripped of the parts that made God the origin of all Being, it said the ways of God are without form. When these things were taken out of the story, there was a collapse of the worthiest part of the origin of man. There came a time in human history when it was more important to control the population than it was to be in the way of God. That said, there are a few parts remaining in Genesis that are worthy of note.

I wish it were possible to know what happened to the story and why people were kept in the dark.

> It's not relevant to this part of the book but I will tell you that it was the beginning of the end of my relationship with the common folk. The keepers of the faith were divided multiple times in biblical history because of the destruction that governments had on the freedoms of human society. It was for the love of power that God has been stolen from the hearts of people. Today it still happens but not as much from government as it is in religions. Religions continue to

argue over the elements of faith, and God is kept out of love's connection to people. But that is for another book, not this one. This book is designed to give God back to the mind of mortal man so that man thinks on his own and maybe, just maybe, finds a way back to me, without consulting a pastor before consulting his own heart.

Okay, sorry for the interruption, we were discussing kinship.

Yes, this is where the kindness of God is relatedness to God. In the time before time, there was a consult of the ways of God.

What does that mean, "a consult of the ways of God?"

Consult is the counsel of the mind. This is where the "we" comes in. The consult of the mind is made up of many.

Many what?

Many minds of God. God is not just one mind, God is made of billions of minds. Each one has significance, and though all of these minds are one God, they each have an area of the universe that is uniquely driven. Each mind is a facet of the single God.

Do they always agree with each other?

Not the way you think, but yes, they are of one mind when it comes to decisions about creation.

How do they disagree?

They disagree with the way that the God realm should conduct its business. But you don't yet fully understand too many things about God to have this discussion. Someday when you are coming back to

God's realm, after you have finished your work on earth, you will get a glimpse of what this means, and that's when you'll get your next assignment.

I will respect the things I have yet to know about God and let the subject rest.

Thank you. It is not easy to control your curiosity because your questions are worthy, but you cannot learn everything about the eons before time in a single human lifetime.

So let's go back to the time before time, in the consult of the mind . . . .

There was a decision to make a mortal man in order to facilitate the nature of God on earth. The answer to the question that you had is that not every mind agreed as to what would be given to the man that the Bible calls Adam. The mind of God chose to give Adam a brain that could memorize all sorts of information before coming to earth so that he would recognize his own kind separate from that which was not his kind. Meaning there were creatures that roamed the earth that had a living soul. These creatures were not like human beings in any sense of the imagination, but they had the source of origin contained within their being. They had, in other words, a soul that Adam could recognize. But instead of agreeing to have this kind of brain, the agreement was instead to allow the Adam to roam free and not be able to recognize soul. That way he could find his own soul without the encumbered spirit that recognizing other souls would cause. The reason these souls would encumber him is because he needed to become the soul of himself, and he would have a difficult time differentiating between himself and other creatures if he saw in them the immortality aspect of God and wondered where he fit into their being.

Can you explain why Adam would not have been able to recognize his own self if he could see the souls of other creatures on earth?

What happens when you are around your cat?

In what way?

What does your cat make you feel?

I feel adoration for him.

You feel love for him, too, right?

Yes.

Well, what if I told you that he had a soul?

Animals have souls?

We're just talking about your cat right now.

If you told me he had a soul, I would wonder about it.

What would you wonder?

I would wonder if his soul knew me.

Right. You would wonder if your soul and his soul were in awareness of each other.

Okay, so?

So what if you were around lots of animals and you could see their souls?

I'm not sure, but I think it would be overwhelming.

You would have a difficult time understanding where the souls leave off and the forms begin. You would need some special form of eyeglasses to filter out the soul in order to see bodies. This is why the counsel decided to make it impossible for Adam to see the souls of the creatures on earth. But it created another problem. Adam could not see his likeness in any of them. He was, in his eyes, the only one of his kind.

Wow. That's incredible. You made it clear to me why kindness is related to finding one's soul.

Yes, well we aren't there yet, but it's okay to jump ahead in your understanding. However, that may have been a glimpse, and I bet you can't explain what you understand.

You're right. It was a glimpse.

It was a glimmer in the effervescent[1] nature of awareness.

Yes.

There's hope for you yet.

Gee thanks, God.

Here's what we know so far. Adam cannot see souls; souls are God's likeness . . . follow me?

Yes, I think you're saying Adam couldn't see God either.

Right. He had yet to discover his heart. He was in search of his purpose right away because there was no world to dictate to him what was important. He just *was*.

How was he put on earth? He wasn't raised by wolves or anything, was he?

> No. That's funny. There is a window that emerges on the world of time that can be passed through, but only from God's realm to man's realm. It is not a window that any other energy level is able to ascend to or descend to in a way that causes Being to have form or shape.

So Adam just appeared out of the clear blue sky?

> Yes, in a matter of speaking. If you have ever been in the ocean, then the creatures of the ocean may have assumed you appeared out of thin air, too.

Wow. Good point.

> So when Adam went in search of his purpose, he was already programmed to take account of all of the creatures he saw. He was to make mental notes, so to speak, so that God could account for the life forms that were emerging from the ether.

Tell me how it's possible you didn't already know what was evolving.

> Well the reason we cannot fully know is because we are not form, and form is something that emerges from the core of being and we are inside the core.

So humans are like computers?

> Yes. That is the best way to describe it.

But we are computers with free will?

> Yes. No two ways about it. The question for your soul, though, is who is programming you? You cannot

achieve free will if you are programmed by the world outside of you, because you become an automaton for the ways of mortal man. You become convinced that the ways with which you see yourself are the ways with which the world sees you. And that is not the case. It is the way you see the world that is the way the world sees you.

So back to Adam . . . Adam was alone; he was not able to discern his own kind. This is where the kindness of God began in mortal humans. Kindness is a connection from the heart and soul where there is giving and receiving, simultaneously. This is where the lifeblood is interacting with spirit form. This is where the connecting tissues of your heart are giving the ways of your being a connection to God.

That is beautiful and so verifiable. I know empirically this is true and wouldn't need science to prove it, because I prove it everyday when I experience kindness from others and when I express kindness toward others.

It is indeed an evidence-based experience as well, because it is a literal occurrence in the body how kindness affects the heart, the blood pressure, the ways of brain patterns . . . there is plenty of scientific measurement possible in the ways of kindness.

This ends another chapter, but I warn you the next chapter is going to be pretty grim.

Chapter 10

The Grim Reaper

When God opens to the world a measure of hope, God also opens a world of death. Hope and death are two doors at the end of every road a man walks down. A man who works his way to the end of the road is a man who is looking for himself. When he finds death he has discovered that the way his life will end is the way life begins anew. When he meets hope, however, he discovers not just his own form of mercy but also God's wish for him to find True Love.

True love is not the way man discovers his worth to mortal man, but his worth unto the way of God. If he stays walking the path of hope, he discovers the riches found in his gestures and his way of speaking to others. If he side-steps hope and turns others into a source of his reckoning, he will see judgment in his own work. This judgment is not going to allow him the fruition he seeks.

What we mean is that when man makes God his path, truth prevails in his heart. When truth prevails in his heart, judging others is left to the source of creation, rather than to worrying about other's misdeeds. Only in hope can a man walk the way of God. Hoping that God has a plan for each and every soul is the only way to relinquish the harm he may do to himself.

It sounds as if you are saying that if hope saves us, it is only when we give others hope and not condemnation that we are in God's way.

> Indeed. But you also wonder what the Grim Reaper is.

Yes. You are hearing my mind.

> When the mind is working, it wouldn't ask the question, it would only seek the enjoyment of the answers.

Well then you heard my thoughts.

> Yes. That is the accurate statement, but we knew what you meant. It is only for the source of God to tell you what you ask for in your thoughts, the mind would only give you an answer you cannot write down. The writing makes it acceptable to the listening part of your brain, where the mind will forget otherwise. The brain will hold the memory until the answer is a learned process of knowing.
>
> Now about the Grim Reaper . . . Look it up.

My dictionary says, "Death personified by a shrouded figure carrying a scythe." Interesting to note the word 'reap' derives from the word ripe.

> Notice that it is death *personified*. As if you are being *taken* from life.

Yes.

> Well, that is essentially what happens. Your spirit is falling away from the body and takes life with it.

Why do you say falling away and not rising away?

> Because falling away indicates there is a letting go
> of the grip. Whereas rising away infers there is a fall-
> ing away of the body. Is this an important distinction?

Yes.

> Well, it's only important when the way of God is
> acknowledged in this event. The way of God is to give
> form life, but when form no longer serves a purpose,
> the way of God is to end the life of form. This end
> is the beginning of a new life in spirit. The spirit has
> many alternatives and the soul is only given one.

You may have already talked about this, but I have forgotten
. . . how is soul and spirit different at the point of the body's
death?

> Refreshing your memory is not a problem for me
> and actually gives me an opportunity to instruct you
> on the grim ways of the soul.
> The soul is a mortal event. Meaning it has a
> choice to live eternally with God or to move toward
> the realm of man. The realm of man has two opportu-
> nities for the soul. One is to re-enter the form through
> another life or enter the world in no form. The later is
> not recommended and should be avoided whenever
> possible. Here's why.
> When the soul does not join spirit, it is lost. It is
> literally, not figuratively, lost. We've explained before
> why the soul gets lost and what the danger of being
> lost causes. Being lost causes the mortal soul to
> remain attached to the past and to never live again,
> if it is not given a chance to join spirit. It can only join
> spirit at this point, if it is made whole, if it is prayed
> for, and if we are given notice of its remembrance.

In other words, you have the power to help a mortal soul to work through the realm of spirit, if that soul wishes for help. When the soul remains in the past it is not capable of knowing itself without a great deal of work on the part of the living. This is a dangerous game for the living to play, however, because the soul that is lost in the abyss is able to attach to objects and to people without full awareness of its predicament.

My question is, what are they experiencing? Is it darkness?

Indeed, but not darkness in the way of something evil, unless it is an evil presence, but most souls that are trapped are not evil, they are just sad and lost and tormented by their own ineptitude.

The definition of inept means "unsuitable to the purpose; unfit." I needed to look it up because I don't see how you're using the word for a lost soul.

Ineptitude is their manner of being. They cannot perform any function. They cannot live-out any purpose, they are stuck between realms and may often lash out at humans as a result of what the ineptitude causes in them. Some have enough energy and force to do damage but not enough to actually get them from the realm of God's work to the world of man.

You mean creative power when you say "God's work?"

Yes. They cannot do anything of any significance. If they passed into the realm of lost souls, they may have plenty of company, but this presents no solace because of the sadness that is everywhere in that realm. The sadness is perpetuated by adding numbers, whereas if they remain alone, a soul is less likely to remind itself of its sadness.

But what I want you to know, and your readers to understand, is these souls are savable. They are able to revive their own manner of hope if you are willing to reward them with kindness.

Kindness is the way to remind them that there is a purpose to their being. If purpose is discovered, the next thing to happen is forgiveness. Forgiveness is what lends them the notion of spirit. The notion of spirit is reclaimed when the soul is able to forgive itself.

Can you give an example of how that works?

Yes. We enjoy examples very much. We like how they make you understand.

The soul that rests inside *your* being is enlightened. You became enlightened when you let go of your control on your life and allowed me to guide and direct you with a sense of purpose. Purpose is the same as intention and the same as direction. Each set of principles that guide direction is what you live by in order to allow me to guide you.

Surrender, joy, and forgiveness are the three principles that make you enlightened. You surrender your mind, you make joy of your work, and you forgive yourself when you fail to measure-up to the perfection you expect from yourself. These are the most important manners of an enlightened soul.

Now, an *unenlightened* soul has what you would consider positive traits in a human being, but is actually *self*-destructive to the mortal soul:

1. Making the will of the individual the primary course of life's only way (the opposite of surrender).

2. What is in the heart is an over-rated message and shows weakness if worked on too much.

3. When the ways of work are hard, there is reward in the form of survival.

Here are three measures of worth that make a mockery of the soul. Can you guess which one causes the soul to be unforgivable to itself and to others?

Number two?

That's right, the heart. The heart is the most misunderstood muscle of the entire body. The heart is believed to be an emotional trigger, but it is not a trigger; it is the source of being and the heart is an indicator of how being is wayed in the body.

I think it might be helpful to clarify "way" because I see what you mean in my mind's eye, but the language is not normal usage. How do you mean "way" as an action of the heart?

The heart works to bring blood through the body and it does so through the ways of the body.

Way here means vessels, arteries, veins, etc.?

That is the literal transportation aspect of way. But there is the figurative and metaphorical as well. Let me explain. The literal is the body and how it behaves. The figurative is the symbolic representation of way, such as the road you walk down is a way, and then there is a metaphorical representation of the ways of the heart as in the heart in your hands.

Like she has my heart in her hands?

Right, but that is figurative. A metaphorical interpretation means that the "heart's ways" represent the "ways of man."

Okay.

So when the heart *ways* the worthier parts of itself, it makes the creative power of God throughout the system. If, however, it is not considered important and becomes ignored or pushed aside, it is made then into a worthless, good-for-nothing mind in the body of the individual. The individual not only pushes out God and his or her own needs, but he or she pushes out the spirit of God in the notion of the Self.

So, how you must interpret the heart is how you must interpret your own being. If the heart is irrelevant, then your being is made irrelevant. There is no two ways about it. The heart is everything when talking about the mortal soul. If the heart is lost in never-ending uselessness, then the soul has nowhere to go but to remain on earth without awareness of spirit. Spirit is God in the manner of God's being that remains in the individual. So when the body returns to the earth, the spirit returns to God and the soul evolves or it does not, depending on the heart of the person who passes. In other words, where the heart goes the body follows. Therefore if there is nowhere for the heart, there is nowhere for the spirit, for the body has been banished from life as the spirit is snuffed out of the heart of the manner of being.

I keep imagining the moment the heart stops. Is this the moment of passing for the soul or the spirit?

When the heart stops in the body, it is merely creating the window of opportunity for passing to the next realm. It does not represent the end necessarily for the individual's life. When the heart no longer functions, it is merely a passing from one phase of being to the next.

So where does forgiveness fit in?

Forgiveness is the nature of giving to the mortal soul a remembrance of worth. Without forgiveness, there is no worth for the soul. When forgiveness is expressed it is a surrendering to the will of spirit, and the spirit works to give life to the soul by taking it to the realm of God. That realm is multilateral, meaning there are many, many levels of knowing that the spirit evolves to. The spirit can lead the soul to the ways of immortality, but not all levels of immortality are worthy to the soul. The soul must cleanse itself of the past first.

Cleansing the past means there are attachments the soul must overcome, before ascension can occur. The attachments to the earth are related to loved ones that are still on earth. If the spirit of the individual is taking the life of its past into account, it may wish to wait for its loved ones to join it before moving on. This is not a bad thing, but it does encumber the soul's evolution from moving into the phases of its own purpose. However this is for another book; let's get back to the saving of the mortal soul from a destruction of spirit.

Spirit cannot be destroyed in itself, but the *link* to spirit can be destroyed if the heart is given no meaning in the life of the soul while it is on earth. This link to spirit is greatly enhanced when the mind of God is acknowledged in the life of the mortal being.

God, can we back-up a bit to the time when the soul enters the body at birth?

Well if you think it would benefit your understanding; that will be a perfect way to talk about the matrimonial course of the soul and body to spirit.

Matrimonial?

Look up the word and we'll work from there.

I don't see anything unique about the word except some mention in the Latin origin related to "mother."

> Indeed, this is a word that has meaning beyond its modern use. What we mean is that the word once carried weight as an aspect of nature; one that "combines over" the cause and effect use of the ways of mother. This way of use is matrimonial.[1]
>
> What we want you to notice is that *in the combining of soul and spirit*, one begets the other. Soul is born out of spirit, the body is born out of soul, the body emerges from the womb, and the womb embodies the way of man. Does this make sense yet?

Sort of—if I look past the modern use of matrimonial, which is an adjective related to marriage.

> The marriage of husband and wife is the matrimonial manner of man and woman in the human society; in other words, social combining. We are using the term to understand what happens when soul and spirit unite. What is the working-way of this union?

The working-way of soul and spirit uniting—can I have a clue?

> The soul and spirit unite for what cause?

To create being?

> By what way are they creating?

By the way of God?

> Yes. This is the answer. God is the working-way of soul and spirit marrying to create being.

God becoming?

>Yes. God becoming.

For what purpose?

>Exactly. What purpose is God becoming?

To know God's Self?

>That will be the outcome, but why is God becoming?

Because God asked, "what am I?"

>Yes, but why is the soul and spirit uniting for the purpose of God to know God's Self through this question, "what am I?"

Because it is God's nature to create?

>But *why* is the soul an aspect of that creation?

Is it a co-creating being?

>Yes! This is the course of becoming, through co-creating being. Now, why is the body an important adjunct to this co-creating?

The body expresses the co-creation?

>No, not exactly. What is the body to the soul?

You said before that the soul puppets the body.

>Yes.

So the body is the manner of the soul?

>Yes. So what is the way of matrimonial work?

The soul and spirit unite to make the body?

What is it they are making?

God on earth?

That's not exactly where I'm going with this line of questions.

Where the soul lives within the spirit is a level of magnitude, and the body is a manner of magnitude that levels-out the construction of spirit. The body is a manner for the soul to exist, on a level of the Self as it makes its own course, once it has entered the realm of man.[2]

So the body is the free will of the soul?

No and yes. Yes in that it says to the soul "this is your way, this is who you are expressing yourself to be." The spirit is that which allows this to occur, because the soul has no creative means of its own. It cannot create form without spirit.[3] To annihilate the spirit's course, once the body has made its way through the maternal system, the spirit must forgo any involvement with the soul, until the soul finds its purpose for becoming. The body enables the soul to become, as well as helps it to unite again with spirit.

So the only way for the soul to accomplish free will is to forget that the spirit exists?

Yes.

But in order to save the soul from becoming lost, the body must acknowledge the soul?

Yes. And then we've already discussed the soul's ability to protect the body, but what else does the body have to do to make the soul complete?

Surrender to the spirit?

Not only surrender, but also to forgive its own unforgivable nature.

What is unforgivable?

Every individual has different degrees of an unforgivable nature. Each soul is in a process of evolving, so each soul is forgiving something different.

I see.

So that which is "held onto" in the heart and not given-up to spirit is what is carried over into the realm of the Grim Reaper.

Will you define your term "Grim Reaper?" The term grim comes from the middle to old English term, grimm: to make a loud sound, roar angrily, "thunder and grumble." My dictionary also says hard and unyielding; relentless, stern; resolute. I didn't know these were the meanings of this word, grim.

Yes. The grim aspect of the Grim Reaper is that which is "unrelenting," representing that which cannot surrender. The problem is not that the soul's heart will not let go to surrender; the problem is that this soul will not let go of its position as overshadowing the good. In other words, if you asked the soul why it is not giving up, it would not say because it doesn't want to let go, it would say that it cannot let go because that would mean it was wrong. And admitting to being wrong is what will cause the problem in the soul's identity. If it believes it is right for whatever reason, and yet admitting to being wrong is what is holding it back from its progression in spirit, then there must be some way to help this lost soul misidentify the problem first, rather than misidentify itself. This means that when the overshadowing of good happens, the unrelenting grim nature is to steal away the soul. But the soul is never stolen away for real; it is forever learning its own course of the natural evolution of the soul.

The soul must evolve to ever greater states of magnitude in order to reach its destiny, but it could take the soul thousands of lifetimes before waking up. So the reaper represents that which steals away the life of the individual. The way the character of the Grim Reaper is revealed to the soul, then, is that of unrelenting sorrow and the stolen life of the soul. The soul is stolen from its *course*, not its sorrow of heart; it is stolen from its course of becoming the nature of God that gives.

Is this the end of the chapter?

One more thing. What is your soul if it is not God?

How can it not be God?

Exactly. It is God. And every aspect of God that is lost is man's responsibility to recover. Remember when we said man was created to account for nature?

Yes.

This is a new aspect of nature that was created when man was created. This is part of your purpose on earth; recover the lost souls that need returning to God.

I guess you're going to be helping this effort?

I always have.

One last question. When do the soul and the spirit enter the body?

This is an abortion question, isn't it?

I guess so, yes.

Well, it's not a good topic to discuss because you will be damned either way by the court of mankind. Let me just say life always finds a way.

That's what I believe.

I have given you that belief because you understand the eternal nature of heaven and the ways of nature to move with eternity. Whatever your soul decides—to live or to not live—is what will be.

So the soul lives before birth?

Yes, and it won't die just because there is no body to be born into. It will find another portal and live where it is brought into the world.

The next chapter is about finding your way back to the source of being and how others can find it too.

Chapter II

The Time Before Mortal Man

There was a time in the history of the earth when mortal man was not even a speck of knowing. Meaning we were not ready to create the earth with man's presence until the time was right. Before the time was right, there was a nature's conquest that had to be done. This conquest was that of great eruptions of skies and great manners of land mass creation. The land was moving and flowing and evolving, and the skies were full of ash and soot and mostly made up of harsh chemistry, unfit for any worldly ways such as the life of humans and mortal natures.

The first creatures to walk the earth were creatures that could survive the climates and chemicals. They were creatures with unbridled natures. They had skin and bone and hair, but it was not what you consider coarse or unruly. The hair was fine and thin and full of bugs that would eradicate the effects of sulfurs and dioxides, and these bugs had all sorts of other worthy abilities. They did not survive the evolutionary ways of a clean environment, however, because they starved without the world's odors. The ways of the earth were very different from today. The caustic air was fuel for these creatures, and they ruled the earth for thousands of years. Unfortunately, their remains were completely crushed in the soil far below the cretaceous period.

The way of working that should help you understand why this is important is to know—that mortal man can do more harm to the environment than he even believes, because simply by changing the balance he is directing the course of Earth's evolution. Evolution and Earth will survive without him, but he will take the earth backward in its course.

What existed on Earth, before mankind, adapted to a far harsher climate than man could create, but *effects* in the proper course take thousands of Earth years to make happen. There are so many concerns about what mortal man has done to the seas and the air, the trees and the earth, in a mere 100 years, that it's impossible to imagine the earth recovering in time to save the mortal mind.

God, doesn't all nature have mortality?

Yes.

So you are saying all of nature is on the brink of destruction?

No. Mortal mind is that which dies in the mind. Nature does not have the illusion that it will die.

Why not?

Because nature knows that what lives will never die because what dies comes back over and over and over. That's how nature sees itself.

Why aren't we seeing it that way?

Because you feed the illusion of death.

So how does that mind affect the planet?

That's not your question. Your question is what does mortal mind have to do with the nature of man, when it comes to destruction of the earth's resources.

Right, that works for me.

You're funny. Okay here goes. The mortal nature of man is in the way he perceives himself. He sees himself as living and dying. He sees "new babies" and he sees birth. He sees "no babies" and he sees extinction. So he keeps having babies. He keeps making babies and keeps making babies. These babies are going to choke off every living thing on this planet until he has no more food for these babies. Then he stops making babies and starts planting resources.

As he plants, he refreshes the systems in nature. Each system feeds another system, and the work that is produced makes a new Earth, a clean resourceful Earth. This is the story of human kind forever. Humans have no idea they are linked to nature in such a big way.

So we need to stop making babies?

Well, that's a start. Humans who think every child is a gift from God do not understand the free will of man. The only gift I gave was the ability to reproduce. The rest is your responsibility. Everyone who *feels* the gift of a child *must* raise a child, because it is seeing the child with purpose that leads that child to its Self. But not many people see a child as a gift; many see a child as a burden.

This is more common, I'm sure.

It is.

But of the people who honestly feel like the child is a gift, a blessing, are you saying that is not real?

> The gift is the perception of something having been given. That is the gift. This is preceded by a child-soul that wanted to give. Even to a family who was not ready for a child, the gift came from the soul who gave, not from me directly. I try to persuade where I can when asked, but ultimately it is the soul's decision to go or not to go to fulfill a human wish for a child.

This chapter is about time before mortal man. What else do you want to discuss about that?

> We're getting to it, just follow along, you're on the path.
> The ways of Being state that if man becomes his own, he will become the everlasting nature of his maker. So if there was a time before mortal man, and this time existed before the earth could hold his inhabitance, what is the time before man?

The natural course of nature to make man?

> No.

I don't know.

> Just try to imagine how nature works. What is it doing?

Balancing the environment?

> No.

I'm remembering science class and having learned that nature produces and consumes.

Right. It produces and consumes; each member of the natural evolution of species is producing or consuming in a balance directly proportional to its existence. That which consumes modifies that which produces. That which stops producing modifies that which consumes. So what if I told you that the time before man, nature was producing and consuming to create an environment suitable for man?

Then humans are reaching their own destiny?

Well, in a short answer this is true, but remember his purpose is to account for nature, so how does that fit into his destiny?

When he sees himself in nature?

Correct. When what man sees in nature is his only way of being, then he becomes balanced within its course. What if he doesn't see himself in nature?

Then he is at its mercy, and he no longer has the will to save nature because it is the enemy to be conquered.

True, but that's not our message. We will devise a scenario to help you understand. The truth in all being lies in a simple wave of being. This simple wave is that of peace; it is a tranquil state of knowing that all is in perfect order, the way it was intended.

That's a beautiful idea, but I keep picturing bulldozers and paved roads, smog and skyscrapers, and billions of energy-hungry lives. Is this what was intended?

Yes. But it's moving faster than nature can keep up. Nature is moving at a slower pace than mortal man's invention. This is the whole point of this book, so in order to quell the progress of mortal man's equipment, the nature of God will step in to minimize man's effect on the earth.

You mean destroy us?

In a sense, yes. Not destroy the earth but destroy man's destructive measures. Man must slow down and show some restraint in how he is making the earth bend to his will. If he does not, the producer/consumer balance will be over-powered by man's greed.

The greed that is making this lack of resourcefulness will upend the ways of man irrevocably. The way you are imagining this is not what we intend. You imagine famine and war and fire and hell. We are not so destructive to the earth. We can more easily destroy progress through illness than through war. There are destructive measures that will end the course of life as you know it. These measures will only serve to slow man down and give nature a chance to catch up.

Is this book a warning? Is that why it's being written?

No, this book is being written to save the souls who will be lost in the course of this destruction.

So the destruction is going to occur?

Yes.

There is no way out?

Yes, there is. If man can irrevocably destroy himself, he can also irrevocably[1] create a new life. If all of the consumer minds fade out and the producer minds emerge, then the production of earth-saving methods will emerge in the minds of mortal man; he can begin to erase the damage he has done by making the toil of man into the toil of saving the earth from destruction. But I know that is not going to happen because I see the souls of those responsible for perpetuating this course and they are not enlightened. They are not for the benefit of nature, nor for the benefit of human-kind, they are for their own wallet.

Has there been a time in human history where this has occurred before?

Many times.

So humanity survives?

Yes, there is a balancing that happens, but this is not one of those times. We already described what is different about now.

Is it because we poison our food supply?

Yes, that's exactly right, and what is really trou-bling about this is that so many innocent people have no idea that this is happening; none whatsoever.

It reminds me of cigarettes before it was discovered they cause cancer.

Indeed, it is exactly the same cover-up, but when it hits the soil and food supplies, then the people who eat the fake food die of cancers for no known reason. There will be hell to pay when they find out the cause.

Is that the end of the chapter?

Not quite, there is one more idea to impart. In the time before man, there was a yearning that caused God to make man a mortal being and not an everlasting being. That yearning was to experience many types of existences.

In this existence, for example, you experienced the life of a young woman in search of her talents. In the last lifetime you experienced being a man of great wealth and great worth in the mind of human beings who knew you. But you were not a kind man, you were in some ways an evil man who was evicted from every bed you entered because of your temper and lashing out at women.

Was I violent?

Not physically, but verbally you were very cruel.

Why are you telling me this? It hurts my heart.

That's what happens when you learn the lessons of God's nature. You surrender to the will of kindness.

Is that why I wanted to be a woman in this life?

Yes, it is also why you were born into a working class family. You needed to know the fruits of labor and the backbone of your worth. You had repented in the last life and knew you had debts to pay, and believe it or not, you paid them all. You have surrendered and paid to those who needed to know that life is good and worthwhile. Now your job to fulfill your duty has been done in this lifetime. You can rest well knowing that the next lifetime will not be on Earth. I will now show you how to make others also capable of this repentance.

That makes me happy.

Chapter 12

The Effects of Goodwill on
the Souls of Mankind

The mortal soul has an alternate mind separate from that of the everlasting mind. The mortal soul is dependent upon the idea that there is a beginning and an end to everything that is. The reason it depends on this cycle is because it needs to learn the course of its own being, and the mind that has no end knows no course, only its Being as being never-ending.

The human mind takes into account all of its nature at once, without learning it has a way of being that allows God to work within the realm of knowing. The realm of knowing is past, present, and future simultaneously. So if the course of human kind makes a shift in any one of the three portals of time, there is a change that affects the other two. The effects in the other two time continuums will represent the nature of all matter and all being.

Okay, this is a difficult set of statements for me to understand because, of course, I am a human mind and so are our readers. So where do we begin to break it up so that it is more understable?

Here's the first clue: One.

One?

Yes, that's the clue.

The realm of God is one time?

Nope. It's true, but not the point of the passage.

Let's start with mortal mind.

Good start.

Mortal mind perceives beginning and end in order to experience the course of its being.

Good.

If it did not perceive the beginning and the end, it would not be able to break away or individualize the course of God being.

Right.

A mind that has no end cannot know the course of its being, because it carries all-time within its being.

You were closely aware but missed an important clue.

What clue was that?

That God knows all being—past, present, and future—because past and present *are* the future.

Is that because of the laws of cause and effect?

No. It is because there is no other alternative but to make the future out of the past. You cannot gain insight on the future if the past is hidden from you. Here's the way of our mind on this point. When God makes the wave of being a future, what happens to the past being?

It is overcome?

> No, but close. It is overshadowed. There is no perception of the past when the future arrives. It is impossible to arise out of something when the mind is taking its cues from the past. Otherwise it is just a reiteration of the past.

So, for example, when medicine discovered the existence of germs, sanitation was then part of the future course, and the eradication of germ-causing illnesses took hold.

> You got it. So the future of mankind became quickly advanced when microbial invasion was discovered.

Yes.

> So what happened to the past?

I don't know.

> You *can't* know because you don't experience the past. But I do. The past still exists in the realm of no time.

So what happens to it?

> The past literally changes course and the future is affected.

How so?

> In the future germs are bigger, more able to withstand the human eradication.

That's frightening.

No, it's not really, because this future is also a past.

How?

There are no germs in the future of this past.

Please explain.

It's not important, nor is it perceivable by humans on earth. It is merely a learning for the creative being. But the reason it is part of this book is because it is a glimpse at how nature works on earth.

Since nature knows no end or beginning, it is capable of teaching itself to survive any course of human awareness.

Awareness? How do you mean that here?

Human mind is human awareness. Human mind will make grave errors but also make intensely fascinating creative measures. So when human mind is creating survival for itself, nature will also find survival for itself in the change of its being to survive. Nature establishes many more devices for survival than man does for his own survival, because he is distracted by making money and making babies. He is distracted by television and media entertainment. He is distracted by the "pursuit of happiness," which is a terribly misguided endeavor; man will never discover happiness outside of his own being.

Back to the conversation about time: Time is very important to grasp in this age of reason, because it is the sole manifest of evolution.

Evolution creates time?

Yes. Evolution is time-driven, but in a unique sense. It is driven by the cycles of nature and the movement of planets. Evolution is a time-driven equivalent to manners of the most-high creative manner. This means that the highest creative manner of God is the highest creative manner of nature, which is called evolution on Earth, but in my realm it is merely the way that creation is working its ways.

Evolution, although time-driven, is equal to the creative power of timelessness?

Yes. Good place to get back to the topic at hand. Time manages all manners of evolution by way of planetary movement. The manner of movement is a time-driven course in itself. When time is in its own being, the realm of knowing is also in its being. Time is not the clock; it is the cycles of everlasting worth.
What is your question?

What is "time's own being?"

Good question. Time is a being that can discover itself. It is capable of discovering its *Self*.

Can you give an example of that? Because I think of time as an abstraction, not an animated thing.

The abstraction is the perfect way of thinking about time in the mortal sense, because there is no way to calculate time in the world of God. The world of God's nature doesn't have time, so there is an abstracted version of it on earth. But, and this is a big but, there is a living, breathing aspect of the time that represents the nature of the movement of God in cycles of its own way. Let me explain as best as I can, but this is not a concept one should take lightly in a reading of this book. This will take some people over many lifetimes to fully grasp.

When the cycles of time began—the big bang—the way that God forgot the ways of the past was through the enormity of the way that cycles expanded the universal laws of being. Meaning, where are the cycles of time heading?

I don't know.

Right, how could you? But you expect me to know, right?

Well, yes.

Well I don't. The way to *know* is only to be aware or conscious of that aspect of the knowing of the universe, and the calculations that that would require are larger than the capacity of the oneness of God to allow, in order for an answer to become apparent.

That means the question would have to spread through the universe, calculations and processing would have to take into account all of the past that ever was and then return the answer to the original source of the question before the oneness of God forgot the question.

RIGHT! How did you understand that?

I created a miniature picture in my mind of the universe and then imagined how sometimes I do that myself. I forget the question I asked myself in the process of discovering the answer. Like digging through my purse and forgetting what I'm digging for.

Well that was a good picture for you then, because that is a symptom of how you are going to make it through the gauntlet of time's rewards. We'll discuss that at a more relevant point in this chapter. But I want to also give you an example of where humans misinterpret the cause and effect principle.

When cause is interpreted by some set of circumstances that are irrelevant to the outcome, the outcome relies on the nature of cause. When cause is no longer its own course, this means the effect is unknown. In other words, if there is a set of circumstances that arise out of nowhere, then what happens to the outcome?

The outcome is unknown?

Yes, but what happens to it?

Something completely unexpected occurs?

Yes, but what happens to the outcome?

It changes course?

Yes! Exactly. So if nature already has a cause and effect principle built into its evolution, then what happens to evolution?

It doesn't evolve?

No.

It evolves into an unknown course?

No.

It goes off course?

Yes! If evolution is a time-driven cycle of events led by the natural course of creative being, then the evolving principles are thwarted by unrelated events. Man has set up a course of de-evolution simply by taking into his being the opportunity to recreate nature on earth.

Are you saying man has over-stepped his bounds in evolution?

> No, we are saying that the effect will cause him and nature to de-evolve. The de-evolution of man is in his unwillingness to understand the course of evolution. The course of evolution cannot be messed with without purpose and expect to have a positive result for the ways of human existence.

So you are not condemning science for playing God, but you are warning man that he doesn't know enough to be doing what he's doing?

> Yes. That is the crux of this communication. So if man wants to make babies, he is going to have to stop making mad science or these babies will have no life worth living.

But isn't science just replicating your nature by creating?

> Of course. That's why we are not condemning, we are more proud than angry, but like a child in the kitchen with a toy, if she moves too close to danger you will move her out of the course of that danger before she gets hurt, will you not?

Yes.

> Man is playing in God's kitchen, and if he doesn't look up and start devising his purpose, he is going to get a boiling pot on his head.

I see. So about the title of this chapter, where does goodwill and the souls of mankind fit in?

Well we're getting there, but there is still more prep to do.

Prep in the kitchen, so to speak.

Indeed. The kitchen is a perfect metaphor to the warning this book is giving. In the kitchen there is a pantry where all of the ingredients for cooking are stored. There is also food in the refrigerator that has need for preservation or it will spoil. This metaphor will only go so far, so forgive us when we have to start mixing metaphors. Just try to keep up.

I will!

The pantry holds the ingredients that if not cared for properly will also spoil. But those preservation techniques are losing their effect because the microbes work in a new environment now. They are now uncovering their own manners of survival. When these microbes are eradicated by the measures of man, there are measures that have not been taken to explore other mechanical effects on preservation. In other words, the preservation techniques in themselves must be updated in order to completely make all food preserved. The reason this is important is not because of harmful bacteria but because good bacteria in the body is being washed away by the over-use of cleansing techniques in the food that is grown.

There are bacterial walls in earth-grown food that are being torn down. These walls keep out harmful bacteria and other microbes. When the walls of this manner are removed, there is limited protection in the cells for mishap. Mishap occurs when not all of the nutrients are available to the cellular system of immunity. Immunity is a huge aspect of creation, and in evolution without immunity there is no system of governance for the cells. Cells work on the nature of immunity in order to devise the manner of self-awareness. Do you see where we are headed yet?

Not really, but I am imagining immunity to be a way of self-awareness from a soulful sense.

In what way?

Well, I imagine a cell to represent my being. And in order to be self-aware, I have to close myself off to invasion against my being—like mean people, for example. I am self-aware and therefore internally focused, and so I look at them and smile rather than giving them the ability to wreck my morning.

This is a perfect metaphor for the importance of immunity to the nature of creative being. You cannot create what you will, if what is willing itself upon you overtakes your state of being. The same is true through the body. Each cell is completely dependent on its state of immunity to function as it is intended.

Okay, so that's one issue with the nature of food in the kitchen. Another has to do with the case of being over-fried.

Fried food?

Yes. It's the most destructive way of making food because it kills off all of the nutritional value in food. Think about it. What could possibly survive a vat of boiling oil?

I don't know.

Trust me when I say nothing survives, absolutely nothing. The taste is preserved, I guess you could say, but that is all.

So, we should not make fried foods.

> None. Not even fried chicken in a pan, the way your grandparents made it.

Aw man, that hurts. There are few foods that come close to giving me a sense of joy the way my Grandma's fried chicken did.

> That's because you gathered as a family and shared joy, not because of the chicken itself.

Huh. No wonder I could never replicate it. I thought I was doing something wrong.

> Well, now you know how the soul is infused with memory.

Really?

> Yes. Food and joy are never removed from the soul of memory. But let's get back to nutrients and man's misguided attempts to improve agriculture. The most important message here is immunity. When immunity is thwarted, all havoc is wreaked against the properties of cellular nutrition.
>
> The abundance of nutrients going into the soil is taken up by the plants and used for food. If the plants are starved for nutrition in the way of a fruitful return, then the fruits of the plant are also made free of nutrients.

But I thought nutrients were added to the soil?

> They are, but they are not good for you to eat. They make healthy looking plants that reverse the effect of herbicides. The herbicides are less necessary because the crops are resistant to the microbes and

insects that feed on the plants. The problem is that the reason they are resistant is because the nutrients these things are feeding on are gone. In other words, there is less actual *food* in the food.

So herbicides are better than genetically modified foods?

In a sense, yes, but even herbicides have terribly negative effects on the systems of the body, so you are trading one danger for another.

The way to reduce the effects of nature on crops is to make the soil resistant to strains of vegetation that draw the insects in. They are drawn in by the decaying plants, not by the growing plants. So if you keep out the decaying plants you reduce the bugs.

But how do you do that?

There are ways to make food in enclosed environments that have strains of nutritional value added to the soil without making the plants resistant to bugs. This is not for this book to cover because you are not an agriculturalist. If you were, we could help you devise a new method of agriculture. We will have to work with someone else who is willing to work with the mind of God. We only hope they read this book and get really curious.

Fingers crossed.

Mine too, but we already know who is going to find this book, so we don't have to cross our fingers, if we had any, that is.

Funny. Now the title of the chapter.

We know it's time to discuss goodwill and its importance to the mind of man's soul. We have

already introduced the way time and evolution are
interconnected, have we not?

Yes.

> Now let's discuss how evolution is connected to
> the soul. The soul is a product of the nature of evolu-
> tion because it exists where man does not, and where
> nature does not. It is the pre-causality of nature.
>
> Soul is the source, or the soil, from which mor-
> tal man has emerged; it is the consciousness and the
> constant-ness. Soul is the course of your being, the
> connection to that which is non-material; it is not
> made of the same building blocks as nature. That is
> why there is a sense that matters of the soul are "un"-
> natural when pertaining to what is deemed "super-
> natural."
>
> Look up the word supernatural.

Supernatural: existing or occurring outside the normal experience or knowledge of man; not explainable by the known
forces or laws of nature; specifically of or involving or attrib-
uted to God or a god." Interesting to note that the word
"super" derives from meaning "over."

> Okay, so there is no mention in that definition of
> something evil or out of the realm of the devil, right?

Right.

> So if we are then to use the term supernatural for
> a case in point, then we should be free of and avoid
> any attack by fundamentalist preachers who believe
> they understand the nature of God above and beyond
> God's own understanding, right?

I hope so, God. I am not comfortable with attacks on my
sense of God.

We know, we are trying to keep you sheltered from that, but you are going to have to build resistance to it because it is unavoidable.

I'll do my best.

Let's get back to the point. Supernatural being means nothing more than "that which is above human understanding," that's all.

Right.

So the soul works in a realm that is above human understanding, at least in this cycle of time. It has not always been that way, but for now we will be advising you in areas that are un-provable by science. You must accept that and not argue with a science-lover about it. Because no one wins in those arguments, everyone loses.

So the goodwill nature of the soul isn't up for debate either. There is enough evidence to make anyone a believer if they want to look beyond their five senses. There are enough manifestations now witnessed on film to at least give pause to a skeptic, if not to completely convince him or her that there is another realm of apparition unexplainable by current forms of "natural causes."

Right, I'm following.

That said, the goodwill of the soul can save humanity from its course of misappropriation of knowledge. This is what we call the modern science world. There is a misappropriation of the knowledge science has been given by the mind of God.

You mean you gave science the ability to manipulate the creative means?

Yes, just as Einstein was given the theory of relativity and Copernicus the nature of the movements of planets. When the asking is clear and the mind is free to move, the answers come as a matter of course.

You mean it is intentional that we are given information about the nature of God's universe?

Yes. Every cycle of human discovery is led by the question of a simple being who wonders. Everyone who wishes to know will be given knowledge, provided they have a clear mind and unrestrained heart. If their heart is led by greed, there will be no way for them to unlock the joy of knowledge because their questions will be tainted.

I see.

So when the genetic code was given to discovery, there was never any intention to use it to manipulate the food for the masses. If that had been the intent, the knowledge would not have been given. But somewhere, someone got greedy, and science is used as a slave to that greed.

I'm sorry, God.

I'm not. It's not a problem that cannot be solved, it's just a matter of whom or what will solve it.

You mean either humans or disease?

Right. It's an either before or after case of involvement for corrections.

Is this where goodwill comes in?

No. No amount of goodwill is going to affect the greedy nature of the humans making decisions about food. The only thing goodwill is going to help are those who will succumb to the diseases that are going to come as a result of this misappropriation. Because if these humans learn that the reason they are sick is because of greed, they will blame others and become resistant to the healthy ways that their body can combat disease.

Within every soul is the power to heal the manners of the body and to heal others, when the sick are made well. If, however, the sick and dying become angry and blame others, there is a danger of passing that anger into their eternal souls, and they will cause a manifestation of their souls that lose the battle against disease of the mind. In other words, "rage into the dying of the light" is not a way to go. Opening the soul to the coming of the light is the only way to save the soul from annihilation.

I don't think annihilation means what people think.

No, it doesn't. Look it up.

To annihilate means to "bring to nothing" . . . from the Latin word nihil, which means "nothing."

Right. Now you're getting it. It doesn't mean destruction in the modern sense. It is worse for the soul than that. It means bringing to the state of nothing-ness. When something that is everlasting is brought to the state of nothingness, that's hell. Here's why.

Have you ever wanted anything so badly that when it didn't happen you were left feeling like you didn't deserve it? You were kept at a manner of giving-up on everything important and went into a deep depression about how you were worthless and undeserving?

Yes actually, I have felt that before.

Multiply that feeling by 100, and that's what hell is for a soul that blames others for its demise. It gets stuck there and the feeling multiplies because it has no other "sense" about it to counter the feeling. When you are a body, there are five senses that are giving you constant feedback in the world. When that feedback stops, the only thing your soul experiences is the loss of a body. When the soul is unprepared for that loss of sensual attraction, then there is an awareness that you do not exist anymore. That lack of existence can be pure joy, if you are prepared to experience a loss of senses.

Losing one's senses is a grand affair for some. For others it is frightening because the awareness of "no thing" is equivalent to non-existence, which means non-equivalence, which means nothing to become. It is the state of "nothing to become" that stops the evolution of the soul. And when the evolution of the soul stops, there is a form of destruction to the mind of *being*.

Why can't the spirit help them?

Because the spirit is not given the right to interfere with the evolution of the soul, unless the soul asks for it. If the soul needs help and guidance from the spirit, and cannot call for it, then it is lost in a state of want without satisfaction.

You mean it may not know that it can ask for help?

Right. If it is in a perpetual state of emotional pain, it will not reach out for help because it believes that what's left of it is all that exists.

So here's where goodwill comes in. If you are in the ways of knowing someone who is passing, and they are not given to fanciful beliefs of soul and spirit, you can assist them by showing kindness.

I think you mean that as more than simple gestures.

I do. You need do more than bring flowers to them in their hospital bed. You can give them a sense of knowing that they have a purpose in the next world. The next world is where they are going. Do not assume they know or accept this. The goodwill manner is simply stating, "You have more to do, I will see you in the next world." That one statement can give them a chance at the asking. If they sense they are lost, there is a chance they will remember your kind words. In that remembrance the soul will ask, "What am I to do next?" That one question is an asking for the guidance of spirit, and spirit can lead them to the evolving mechanisms of hope.

What if they have passed a long time ago and are haunting objects or locations?

Then the same is true. If you can tell them they have a purpose and they must move on to the next stage of their evolution, they will find peace and stop making a nuisance of themselves on earth.

Can I ask one last question?

Yes, you want to know what the gauntlet of time's reward is, right?

Yes!

This is a time in the portion of your evolution that makes you a purposeful being. It is the moment of your awareness that you are going to have a new assignment within the realm of God. It is the moment that you are known to God's greatest wishes for the evolution of mankind. When you go through the gauntlet you will be asked many questions that determine your level of understanding the mind of God; the higher your skill-level the higher your association with the spirit of God. This is a topic we will discuss in another book more fully, if you wish.

This is the end of this chapter and the end of this book. More books will come, but now it's time for you to rest your weary hand.

Thank you so much for the opportunity to be of some small use to you.

You are more than welcome, and we are so pleased to know this information will be given to people who need to know they are not alone.

Footnotes

In an attempt to clarify some difficult passages, I have asked for further explanation and organized the answers here. Some aspects of this work will be difficult for many readers because the ways of nature, and therefore God, work differently from what we have been taught.

Chapter 6

1. *When the world began its manner of searching for the ways of its own making,* [when "the age of man" began asking how humans came to be], *it began a destiny that was foretold. It began a search into the ways of creation by the very struggle of making a worthier life than the one of the worth of God* [this is when man's "knowledge" moved from God doing the creating, to evolution creating, but without purpose, "survival of the fittest" for its own sake; and the age of reason]. *When that search began, there was no God to give the world direction. The world's direction became one of never-ending duty. This duty was in the toil and the toil had no meaning.* [If we do not know that life has a purpose, we seek no purpose for our own lives. We work and work, out of a sense of duty, not purpose.]

2. *One day God decided it was time to introduce the purpose that the world had forgot. In this day there was a mighty wind. This wind was strong and full of destruction.* [This can be interpreted any way in which wind destroys; solar wind, hurricane, etc. No one is targeted, nor is there intention as to who is to be destroyed. Only the forces of nature determine that, not God.]
When calm became the world again, all that was left was a few manners of worldly makings. [Manners of repairing the damage from the winds.] *These few manners were those of rock and stone.* [Rock and

stone symbolize that which will not blow into oblivion.] *What stood before the gentle creatures that survived* [gentle creatures are the people who were humbled by the destruction, those who helped the ones who suffered through the destruction; they were also those who secretly felt that God was making a statement], *was a temple of doom,* [temple of doom is the constant worship of destruction through fear and worry about the future of humankind and the earth] *and in it, were two works from the previous dwellers.* [These are humans of the past; they left the works of the Hebrews and Jesus.] *These works represented the light of God and the darkness of the doom and despair of never-ending sorrow.* [Jesus' message was one of light and Love of God, but many interpreted his legacy as warning of hell and the devil; this is the "never-ending sorrow" of hell.]

3. *When the manners of destruction had made the course of the world into a worshiping work,* [the "course of the world" is what we are asking ourselves now, as we watch the destruction of the earth's resources and fear for earth's future, as well as our own. "Worshiping work" is how we perpetuate an idea within our cultural mindshare], *there is nothing but the remnants of light to lead the new world out of its doom.* [The "remnants of light" are what exists in each of us. We are not only capable of reversing the destruction we have begun, but we are capable of creating a new future than the course we are currently on.]

Chapter 7

1. *the nature of your being could move across the open waves of manner* [This refers to the manner of your being that works through the ways of God. It is how you interact with the forces of nature. You no longer have a body to tell you where you exist, so you exist everywhere that your thoughts will act upon. Your thoughts will move your existence anywhere you wish to exer-

cise them. If you do not wish to move anywhere, then you are left with making a stand where you are. This is not the best plan for your soul, because your soul needs the ever-moving nature of your mind in order to become the more evolutionary balance of your status in the ways of God. This is not easy for anyone to understand; especially when the physical body is all you imagine yourself to be. If you have some aspect of your managed life reduced to a hill of beans, then you will find that you must see yourself as more than these things that have now become rubble in your life, or you will die without the purpose for which you were designed to live.]

2. The "inevitable worth of God" is the way that God creates. In the ways of evolution, God is the substance that formulates each cell's construction. God's ways are in the cell division, one after the other, each cycle of division contains the way that God creates. Therefore, when creation was in the half-Spirit half-body realm, there was a method that God used to move each creature's construction so it produced more of itself. This process was not very easy for which to provide diversity; diversity can only come from passing genes between sets of parents. So when God created beings, one from another, there was a form of cloning happening that caused all of the beings to look so similar that it was difficult to move the process of creation passed its own mirror. This is why God invented male/female. Humans were not allowed the male/female construct for a very long time in their existence, because there was a form of rebellion that God knew was coming. The rebellion would mean God would have to let go of the humans, and until God could secure our survival on the earth, God could not simply allow us to have complete freedom. This is a very long time in the history of human construction. There is no evidence that this ever happened, so this information will have to be taken on faith, or at least allow your soul to hear it fully by letting go of your belief systems.

Chapter 9

1. Effervescent: "giving off gas, bubbling up, foaming up"

Chapter 10

1. God is describing nature as having had only one rule for reproduction and that is the "mother" nature.

2. *Where the soul lives within the spirit is a level of magnitude, and the body is a manner of magnitude that levels-out the construction of spirit. The body is a manner for the soul to exist on a level of the Self as it makes its own course, once it has entered the realm of man.* [This passage describes where the soul exists as a level of its own being, relative to the body and spirit. The spirit is the highest level of magnitude of the three, but the body is the lowest only in order to make a material version of the soul. They are not exact mirrors of each other because the soul cannot do what the body can do. The soul also has ways of doing more than the spirit can do, but it is not able to perform these things without the spirit's okay. The spirit must be part of everything the soul does outside of what the body does. So if there is a reason to travel to other realms, for example, the spirit must come along with the soul or the soul can get lost in the other realms and forget that it has a body to return to.]

3 . . . *because the soul has no creative means of its own. It cannot create form without spirit.* [That a man has not the creative means to make a baby without a woman is similar to how the soul cannot express the creative means without the spirit.]

Chapter 11

1. From the word "revoke," which means to formally cancel something. We cannot cancel the course of the damage that has been done, but we cannot also cancel the course of good we can do.

About the Author

SONDRA SNEED is a science and technology writer for industry, and a former atheist with a secret. All the years she spent interviewing scientists and engineers, translating their high-minded knowledge for lay persons, she has also been interviewing the highest mind, the Creator of the Universe. She is also the author of two as yet unpublished books, *The Real Story of the Garden of Eden*, and *The Meaning of Life's Design.* She lives with her husband and his son in Houston, Texas. Visit her at *www.sondrasneed.com.*

Related Titles

If you enjoyed *What to Do When You're Dead,*
you may also enjoy other Rainbow Ridge titles.
Read more about them at www.rainbowridgebooks.com

The Cosmic Internet: Explanations from the Other Side
by Frank DeMarco

Conversations with Jesus: An Intimate Journey
by Alexis Eldridge

Dialogue with the Devil: Enlightenment for the Unwilling
by Yves Patak

The Divine Mother Speaks: The Healing of the Human Heart
by Rashmi Khilnani

Difficult People: A Gateway to Enlightenment
by Lisette Larkins

When Do I See God: Finding the Path to Heaven
by Jeff Ianniello

Dance of the Electric Hummingbird
by Patricia Walker

Coming Full Circle: Ancient Teachings for a Modern World
by Lynn Andrews

Thank Your Wicked Parents
by Richard Bach

*Hemingway on Hemingway: Afterlife Conversations
on His Life, His Work and His Myth*
by Frank DeMarco

The Buddha Speaks: To the Buddha Nature Within
by Rashmi Khilnani

Jesusgate: A History of Concealment Unraveled
by Ernie Bringas

Messiah's Handbook: Reminders for the Advanced Soul
by Richard Bach

Blue Sky, White Clouds
by Eliezer Sobel

Flames and Smoke Visible
by D. S. Lliteras

Inner Vegas: Creating Miracles, Abundance, and Health
by Joseph Gallenberger, Ph.D.

Rainbow Ridge Books publishes spiritual
and metaphysical titles, and is distributed by Square
One Publishers in Garden City Park, New York.

To contact authors and editors, peruse our titles, and
see submission guidelines, please visit our website at:
www.rainbowridgebooks.com.

For orders and catalogs, please call toll-free:
(877) 900-BOOK.